ST. MARY
BEAMINSTER
A
HISTORY

A. A. G. WALBRIDGE

ST MARY'S CHURCH TOWER

ST MARY BEAMINSTER

A
HISTORY

Alec A. G. Walbridge

Published by Walbridge Publications
Hurst Beaminster DT8 3ES

© A Walbridge 2002

ISBN 0-9544111-0-2

The entire proceeds of this book are devoted to
St Mary's Beaminster Fabric Fund

Printed by Creeds the Printers, Broadoak, Bridport, Dorset. DT6 5NL

They vound a pleace where we mid seek

  The gifts o' grace vrom week to week,

    An built wi' stwone, upon a hill

    A tow'r we still do call our own;

  With bells to use, an' meake rejaice,

  Wi 'giant vaice, at our good news:

  An' lifted stwones an' beams to keep

  The rain an' cwold vrom us asleep.

Our Fathers' Works - William Barnes

CONTENTS

ILLUSTRATIONS

Frontispiece: St Mary's Tower

APPENDICES

ACKNOWLEDGEMENTS

Thanks are due to the Dorset and Wiltshire County Record Offices for making available so efficiently material for research. Thanks are also due to the Dorset County Library for obtaining obscure books often from distant libraries.

Early Days

In considering the history of the church in Beaminster it is useful to review the early days of Christianity in Dorset, which eventually led to the founding of the 'old' Minsters, of which Beaminster was one. The Augusta division of the Second Roman Legion under the command of Vespasian, came into West Dorset, in the middle of the 1st century, they found the local tribe - the Durotriges - living with their animals around the dew ponds of their hill-top settlements and worshipping their Celtic gods. The valleys were filled with thick deciduous forest, traversed with a few trackways, and the lower ground was frequently marsh. The Romans brought improved methods of making roads and in the Beaminster district they established their camp on Waddon hill. During their occupation of 400 years the improved techniques, which they brought, enabled the clearance and drainage of land in the valleys. This, eventually led to a settlement in the valley of the river Brit which is now Beaminster. The Book of the Axe states that there was no Roman settlement as no artefacts were found there. This is totally incorrect. The date of the founding of the settlement is not known but various Roman artefacts found in the area include Roman coins, pieces of Samian ware and typical Romano-British black ware, some with white mica inclusions, - evidence of occupation. Furthermore, Romano-British farmsteads were established, overlooking Beaminster, to the north of the settlement, along the spring line, where the greensand meets the fuller's earth. The sites of two of these farmsteads were reported to the Dorset Natural History and Archaeological Society in 1957.

The first of these, however, at map reference ST476031, Buckham Down, was discovered by the writer in 1935. Purbeck tiles, nails, and pieces of burnished black pottery with incised linear decoration were sent to the British Museum for identification. The Museum confirmed that this was a Romano-British site. The location of these sites was undoubtedly due to the presence of spring water close at hand and the existence of the Roman road, the 'broad road', running east-west along the top of the hill.

Christianity came into the country during the Roman occupation and into Dorset. The earliest reference to Christians in Britain is by Tertullian in the early 3rd century and by Origen thirty years later. The British Christians were represented at the Council of Arles in A.D.314. There are many artefacts which demonstrate the existence of Christianity in several parts of Dorset in Roman times. The two major archaeological finds are the tessellated pavements at Hinton St. Mary and at Frampton. The former was found under a field and the site was excavated by the British Museum in 1963. The mosaic was found to be the floor of a room in a wing of a Romano-British villa. This room was orientated East-West and was 28' 4" by 19' 6". In the centre of the pavement was a roundel with a depiction of Christ against a background of the earliest form of the Chi-Rho symbol. Coins and a window grille found on the site dated the villa as A.D. 270-400. The mosaic was in 13 colours and is now in the British Museum. This is the earliest British representation of Christ and is the first known picture of Christ in a mosaic floor to be found in the Roman Empire. The Chi-Rho was in general use in the 4th century but this early form has been found at a site in the south of France and also in an ancient Coptic church at Dendera in Egypt. This illustrates the degree of communication between countries at the time. Clearly this room was a place of Christian observance, probably a chapel, and the owner was a person of wealth and authority, but not necessarily a Roman. Many of these villas were owned by Britons who had become thoroughly Romanized and very wealthy, by trade.

A similar mosaic was found upon excavating a villa at Frampton. It was the opinion of Professor Jocelyn Toynbee that both mosaics were by the so called Dorchester school of designers. However the Frampton mosaic has much more pagan symbolism as a border. The

The central roundel of the Hinton mosaic with minor damage
restored by computer restoration

image of Christ is in the centre of a large square in the corners of
which are four figures which may represent the four Winds of Heaven.
This echoes pagan practice which goes back to the Middle East where
the image of the god was placed in the centre of the inner sanctum
with four lesser deities in the corners to illustrate that the god was the
centre of all things. A typical example is the misnamed temple of the
obelisks at Byblos in the Lebanon which dated from the 2nd millennium
B.C.

Concern was expressed that Christ should be depicted in a floor, so that in A.D. 427 a decree was made by Theodosius and Valentinian ordering its removal from the floor. However, either the decree never reached West Dorset, or the villas were already disused. A number of other Christian artefacts of the period have been found. A stone bearing the 'fish' symbol was unearthed at Dorchester in A.D.1898, silver spoons and a silver ligula was found which suggests that the Eucharist was celebrated there. At Iwerne a stone inscribed with the cross was unearthed. At the Poundbury Romano-British burial ground some interments were orientated East-West and without grave goods which suggests Christian burials. The site also contains painted wall plaster figures in the 'orans' attitude of prayer.

When the Roman army of occupation left Britain it is very unlikely that all the British Christians lost their faith, and there is evidence that they did not do so. Isolated congregations are known to have existed and there was a Bishop of London as late as A.D.580. St. Birinus, a Frank, began the conversion of the West Saxons in A.D.634. Cynegils, who had come to the throne in A.D.611, was the first Christian West Saxon king. He was baptised in A.D.635.

The Saxon Minster

Beaminster was one of the 'old' Saxon minsters. The exact date of the foundation is not known but the earliest documentary evidence of its existence is a charter by King Ethelred dated A.D.681 in the archives of Gloucester Cathedral. A copy of this in 13th century contracted Latin, together with other Saxon charters, was printed, upon the proposal of the Master of the Rolls and approval of the Lords of the Treasury, in 1857, in what is known as the Rolls series. In the text of the charter is a date (A.D.671) but in the Historia of Gloucester Abbey the correct date (A.D.681) is given yet states that Ethelred is in the 25th year of his reign. This cannot possibly be true since he came to the throne in A.D.675. These are typical clerical errors. At the foot of the charter is a note, thought to be contemporary with Henry VI, "Non curetur de congruitate", (No care taken with consistency). To this John Prynne, an antiquary, had added "Who can say that hee's certain of Times and Faces in Historians?". The charter confirms grants of land for the foundation of Gloucester Abbey. In the case of Beaminster it states, "et adjunxit Etbebing mynster illic et Onport lande ad illiam ecclesiam cxx cassatorum in occidentalibus Saxonibus", i.e. that 120 cassati of land from Beaminster and Portland were being given to endow the abbey.

This charter provides a number of facts about the Minster in Beaminster. Clearly it was not only in existence but well established by the latter part of the 7th century. Furthermore it was wealthy. A cassatus, or hide of land, was normally 120 acres, although there was some variation in different parts of the country. Therefore the gift to Gloucester was 14,400 acres - a not inconsiderable present! It is also quite clear that the Minster was dedicated to St. Bee (variously known as Bebing, Bea or even Bega). There have been many conjectures about the derivation of the name Beaminster but in the 7th century there can be no doubt that it was named after St. Bee. One of the misleading suggestions comes from a student dissertation on place names in Dorset by A. Fagersten and published by the University of Upsala. This has been published and re-published uncritically. It uses the fact that the death of Bishop Wulfsige, who had become bishop of Sherborne in A.D.992, in his manor at Langdon, is recorded in the Vita Wulfsini. This can be found in translation entitled "The Life of St Wulfsin of Sherborne by Goscelin" edited by C.H. Talbot in the Revue Benedictine. His death took place on the 8th of January A.D. 1002 in Bega Monasterium and reads "Regente ergo extrema hora in sela episcopali, uti mos erat, eger collocatus et miserio sancti unctionis insignatus" (Carried therefore at his last hour in the bishop's chair, as was the custom, vestmented and anointed with extreme unction).

However, Fagersten wrongly equates Bega Monasterium with Beaminster. The word monasterium was used for monastic property only. Ecclesia was the term invariably used for minsters or churches. This had been the case since the time of the gospel according to St. Matthew chap. 6 v. 18 where it was first used. It has been suggested that 'bega' is a transliteration of the Saxon 'beag' - a ring. This is to misunderstand the grammar of the Saxon language. 'Bega' is the plural of the Saxon 'began' meaning a cultivation. Bega, therefore, means an agricultural estate. Bega Monasterium clearly refers to the Langdon estate. This is supported by Professors Joseph Bosworth and Northcote Toller compilers of the Anglo-Saxon dictionary. Further the minster at Beaminster was more than 300 years old at the time of the Bega Monasterium estate.

Variations in the spelling of Beaminster have included:- Bebingmynster in the Cartularium Saxonicum, A.D. 872, in the Domesday Book A.D. 1086 and the Book of Fees, A.D.1212 the spelling is Beministre. Hutchins, the Dorset historian, gives both Beleministre and Beymyestre. There have been other even less credible suggestions e.g. John Banger Russell put forward the idea that Beaminster derived from 'beau' (beautiful) because of the tower. This is to ignore the fact that the Minster was more than 700 years old when the present tower was built! The actual site of the Saxon Minster is not known for certain but there are a number of facts which make it highly probable that it was on, or near, the site of the present church.

The present church stands on a outcrop of oolitic limestone and this, in Saxon times, was the highest point in the original settlement. The highest point was often chosen for churches since they were intended to be seen by anyone approaching and were an important icon. Further this site was traditionally a prehistoric sacred mound, although there is no proof of this, and the church builders would have wished to use it to obliterate a pagan site, as they did in many other places. Being a mound of limestone gave the position other advantages.

It was dry whilst the surrounding land was very marshy, traversed by small rivers and rivulets. The limestone also provided a firm foundation which was essential for a large stone building. The Saxons were now building in stone and there was hardly anywhere else in the area where they could safely put their building. For purposes of protection and for the accommodation of the Minster staff the building needed to be close to, or within the bounds, of the town. The site on the mound fulfilled these requirements. The use of high ground for building was following a traditional practice of the Saxons. Most of them had come from the Netherlands, particularly the part that is now known as Friesland. Here from the earliest times they had had to live on natural hillocks, since the surrounding land was often covered with water. Later artificial hillocks were created and this, originally a necessity, had become established practice. A practice necessary in Beaminster since it was often flooded as, indeed, it has been more than once within living memory. The Saxon minsters had a churchyard burial ground. They would not have wished to bury their dead in a marsh so a dry site was sought on those grounds as well. Originally the churchyard was rectangular and about one acre which was typically Saxon and, perhaps, owes something to Roman influence. The late Norman Edwards, architect of Beaminster, made a special study of the site and in his papers, which he left with the present writer, draw attention to the fact that it is tolerably certain that St. Bega's church stood parallel to the north boundary of the churchyard, the site of the present Strode Room. This was because of the imperishable belief, inextricably bound up with superstition, that the shadow of the church must never fall over the graves. Conversely a monolithic stone cross would have stood in the centre of the churchyard for the sun to cast its shadow on the graves around it. This cross would have stood where the south wall of the present tower stands. How widespread this superstition was is not known but there are other examples. The nearest is at Winterbourne Abbas where the wall of the Saxon church is exposed, parallel to the present church, which is along the north side of the churchyard. It should be remembered that the church mound was considerably larger than today. It has been pared away on all four sides over the centuries. No artefacts were reported during these excavations, but if there were any they would probably have gone unrecognised.

The name of the founder of the Minster is not recorded, but the circumstantial evidence points strongly to St. Aldhelm (Ealdhem) as the founder. He was born at Wareham, where his parents owned an estate, in A.D. 639 or 640. His parents had been converted to Christianity by St. Birinus four years previously. Aldhelm from an early age was familiar with the western parts of Wessex. St. Aldhelm was educated in the Benedictine monastery at Malmesbury. There he was taught by Maelduib who had come to England by way of Ireland and converted to the Roman prescription. The Irish saints were honoured in Maelduib's school. Amongst these was St. Bee a saint in the Roman calendar. She was the daughter of a king and a holy woman in Ireland in the sixth century, sometimes known as St. Bea or Bebing. She was veiled a nun by St. Aidan and is patron saint of Cumberland. She is commemorated on October 31st. For a time she occupied a cell near the monastery of Whitby, known originally in Saxon as Streanaeshalch. She was a roving Celtic missioner helping to spread the rudiments of Christian civilisation along the river valleys of south-west England. There is a legendary account of St Bega printed in the Carlisle Tracts from the Cottonian Mss., Faust B. 4, fol. 122-139 recording the exploits of the "Godmother of Beaminster" as Bega became known. It is unlikely that she personally founded the Saxon Minster in Beaminster but her choice as Patron Saint suggests that St Aldhelm may well have dedicated it as the founder. If he was not the founder it is difficult to see who was since we have no other person of such status in the immediate area at that time.

The Synod of Whitby in A.D. 664 settled the dispute between

the Celtic and Roman missions and the church was organised into dioceses. This was, therefore, just the time when the minsters would be founded, not only Beaminster, but Axminster, Yetminster, Charminster and Wimborne Minster. The area which Beaminster administered consisted of some twenty-six settlements which corresponded to the area later known as the Beaminster Hundred with some additional land to the south known as Redhove. A number of these locations are now reduced to hamlets or farms. The settlements were as follows:

Oscherwille (Askerswell)	Axnolre (Axnoller)
Beiminstre (Beaminster)	Erneleys (Benville)
Bovewode (Bowood)	Bratepolle (Bradpole)
Windesore (Broadwindsor)	Bochenha (Buckham)
Catesclive (Catsley)	La Chapele (Chapel Marsh)
Cardesstoche (Chardstock)	Cedindon (Cheddington)
Coriscumbe (Corscombe)	Halghestok (Halstock)
Lahoc (Hooke)	Mapertone (Mapperton)
Melepleychs (Melplash)	Mortestorne (Mosterton)
Niderberrie (Netherbury)	Pickiete (Picket)
Bovrtone (Poorton)	Pedret (South Perrott)
Seweberge (Seaborough)	Stoche (Stoke Abbott)
Tolre (Toller Whelme)	Welle (Wellwood)

At the end of the 7th century, Ine, king of the West Saxons, authorised the new diocese of Sherborne, of which Beaminster became a part. St. Aldhelm became its first bishop. In A.D. 705 Aldhelm founded the cathedral at Sherborne, but on May 25th 709 he died on his rounds in the church of Doulting. He was the first Englishman, as far as is known, to write in Latin verse. He also wrote songs, which were published later in King Alfred's handbook, but none of these have come down to us. Bede speaks of him as a wonder of erudition.

A problem of the early church was to find men who were suitable as priests. St. Aldhelm reproached the priests on three grounds:

1. They did not wear the Roman tonsure.
2. They did not celebrate Easter at the time fixed by the Council of Nicea.
3. They treated the Saxon Christians as if they were no better than pagans.

Even as late as the ninth century King Alfred complained of the difficulty of finding priests who were literate enough to read the bible or the liturgy and he set up schools to correct this. However the problems were not confined to local priests. In the last years of the tenth century King Ethelred gave Wulsige, Bishop of Sherborne, permission to introduce Benedictines there. Thereafter Benedictine priests were used to staff minsters and such was the case in Beaminster. The Benedictines were unpopular and suffered hatred, persecution and even violence. In fact when they were introduced at Gloucester seven were murdered by Wulfin le Rue, a rich nobleman. Gradually the Benedictines spread through the whole church. In 1142 on the recommendation of Gilbert Foliot, the Benedictine Abbot of Gloucester, the see of Salisbury, after a long vacancy, was filled by Joceline a Benedictine. The monks of Cerne had elected Bernard, prior of St Peter's Gloucester as the new abbot, who had been commended strongly to the Pope by Foliot.

During its existence the diocese of Sherborne had few bishops who had ten years in office. The difficulties were due to the fact that the appointment of bishops was a royal prerogative and subject to the whims of the king. A typical example occurred in 1023 when Bishop Brithtwine was deposed to make way for Bishop Aelfmaer. This was said to be a reward from Cnut to Aelfmaer for earlier traitorously betraying Canterbury to the Danes. However Aelfmaer went blind in 1027 and Brithtwine resumed his office.

Some bishops enriched themselves, whilst in office, at the expense of the minsters by annexing land. This they legalised by obtaining a charter from the king. Although these charters are now lost there is a record of some of them. Examples are:- 10 hides transferred from Coriscumbe (Corscombe) to the Bishop of Sherborne by a charter of Cuthred, King of the West Saxons; land transferred from Niderberrie (Netherbury) by charter of King Aethelwulfe; and land at Algestock (Halstock) annexed also by charter of King Aethelwulf.

The Saxon minsters not only conducted a religious ministry but also had a number of other functions. They were juridical in that they had to bring offenders before the bishop's court. They were the social service of their day and later, when staffed by monks, were also the health service. An important duty was the gathering of the taxes. These were known as scots, hence the modern English expression scot-free. This system of taxation gradually developed and by the end of the tenth century was in full use. Of these the tithe was the most important. All men who kept animals or raised crops were bound to pay a tenth of the yield to the church. This was divided into three parts, one for the upkeep of the minster building, one for the ministers and one for the poor. The tithe of young stock was to be paid by Pentecost and the fruits of harvest by All Saints day (1st November). Later the tenth acre rather than a tenth of the crop was allocated to the church. In addition there was church-scot, or first fruits, paid on the feast of St Martin (11th November) in the form of a load of grain per taxation hide or 4d. Plough-alms were a penny for each plough or plough land paid fifteen days after Easter. Light-dues were fees for church candles paid three times a year at Candlemas, Easter and All Saints. Soul-scot was paid at the open grave. Rome-scot, also known as Peter's pence went to the Church of Rome. A further tax, Ship-scot was levied in the Beaminster area. This was, apparently, to support the states shipping. Some of these taxes had to be passed up through various hands and it is known that not all of the money reached its final destination. At the beginning of the 11th century there was a letter from Aelthric, Bishop of Sherborne, to Aethelmaer complaining that he was not receiving Ship-scot from a number of places including Dibberwurthe (Dibberford).

This, of course, was Beaminster's responsibility.

During the Saxon period Manorial churches began to arise in Beaminster area. These were the beginnings of the parishes we know today. They were established by the land owners for their work people. Originally all candidates for baptism had to travel to Beaminster at Easter. The ceremony began outside the church and continued at the font inside. This is what established the tradition of the font being close to the door of the church, which was liturgically its correct position. Candidates were annointed with Holy Water outside the Minster and marked with the cross at the font inside. Eventually the manorial churches became independent and had their own baptismal fonts. Manorial churches had their own graveyards but the Thegns (landlords) were still buried at Beaminster where funerals could be conducted with more ceremony and there were staff to say masses for their souls. Manorial graveyards were for the poor. Thus Beaminster did not lose out on the grave-scot. Only one of the manorial churches became independent during the time of the Sherborne diocese and that was Netherbury. Manorial churches had to acquire and afford clergy. This clearly could take a long time to achieve. As late as 1218 we learn that Mortesterne (Mosterton) received gifts of land by seven donors which enabled the consequent establishment of regular services by a settled chaplain. Sometimes the development was hampered by funds being taken away by the diocese or by monasteries. In 1163, for example, an agreement was made between the Abbot of Sherborne and the Succentor of Sarum acquiring certain tithes of Bromley, a manor at Stoche (Stoke Abbott). On June 6th 1191 the church at Stoche was appropriated to the monastery of Sherborne. It was not until August 24th 1238 that Sherborne gave up collecting dues from Stoche.

In the year 1058 Herman, a priest from Lotharingia and protégé of Queen Edith, who had been appointed Bishop of Ramsbury, was also appointed Bishop of Sherborne. He thus united the two sees. F. Barlow writing in the 'English Church 1000 - 1066' states that under

Herman, Ramsbury was kept in a sorry state and he had apparently 'swallowed up' the churches of Beaminster, Charminster and Yetminster. Herman also attempted to annex Malmesbury but was successfully resisted. Herman stayed in office through the Norman Conquest.

Parishes and Prebends

Parishes as such were begun by the Archbishop of Canterbury towards the close of the seventh century and extended but not completed until the reign of Edward III. From the start the civil parish of Beaminster was quite independent. Beaminster had a separate Vestry meeting which, like all vestries, had most of the powers of the present Parochial Church Council, the powers of the Parish and District Councils, and some of the powers of the County Council. The Vestry also had the power to levy parish rates.

Most churches had a patron who had certain rights of control and particularly the right of advowson. This meant that the patron had the right of choosing a priest and presenting him to be installed as the incumbent of the parish. It seems probable that one of the earliest patrons of the church in Beaminster was the Saxon Bishop of Sherborne, Wulfsige III, who held the manor of Langdon. No documentary proof of this patronage has been found but Wulfsige III died there at the start of the 11th century. In Norman times the Diocese of Salisbury was founded in 1075 and absorbed the Diocese of Sherborne that had existed since A.D.705. In 1091 St William Rufus Osmund, Bishop of Salisbury, who is recorded in Domesday Book as holding Beaminster in 1086, endowed Salisbury with the revenues and knight's fees of Beaminster, Netherbury, Yetminster, Charminster and Alton (Pancras). Up to the late 13th century the surrounding estates belonged to Beaminster. Then prebends were set up. These were areas of land whose dues were designated to support a canon in the cathedral. The prebends of Prima, Secunda, Ecclesia, Terra and Slape did not exist before that time. The first Prebendary of Beaminster was John Polebergham who died in 1297. The first record of Ecclesia, carrying the patronage of Beaminster and Netherbury, was in 1291 when its revenues were worth £60. Parvulus de Monteflorum was holding this when he died in 1329. The earliest records of the other prebendaries show Alexander de Hemingsby succeeding W. Denys at Slape at the latter's death on 16th May 1304. Rob de Winchcombe was prebendary of Terra on May 7th 1311.

It is sometimes assumed that the patrons of St Mary's Church were always lords of the manor or clergy. This was not so. In fact the rights of the patron could even be bequeathed by the holder. A look at some of the early patrons makes this clear. In 1554 Thomas Richard Arscott and Thomas Brown, farmer of the prebendary were patrons. John Strode was patron from 1608 and the patronage was still in that family in 1661. The King became patron in 1662 since the patronage has lapsed. In 1667 John Westcomb and in 1697 Edward Pocock prebendary were patrons. The Prebendary of Ecclesia was William Stevenson patron in 1740 and he conveyed the patronage to George Pritchard of Hereford in 1747. By 1760 the patronage was again vacant and assumed by the Bishop of Salisbury.

From Sherborne to Salisbury

In the year 1075 the Council of London required bishops to settle their seats in large rather than small places. Shortly after Bishop Herman translated his see to Old Sarum being nearer to the capital Winchester. The cathedral at Sherborne reverted to being an abbey. The abbot of Sherborne then became a canon of Sarum. Sherborne Abbey was dissolved in 1538. In 1078 Herman died and was succeeded by William Rufus Osmund, who later became a saint. Osmund immediately set about organising common worship throughout the diocese. To this end he produced a document "Tractatus de Officiis Ecclesiaticis", later generally known as the Register of St Osmund. This is considered the most treasured of all the muniments in the registry of the bishops of Sarum. However the present document in the archives is not the original. It is a copy made between 1215 and 1230 when the new cathedral at Salisbury was being built. It is in 13th century contracted Latin on vellum. In its reference to St Osmund it states 'felicis memoriae' (of happy memory) which shows that it was copied after St. Osmund's death. (See Appendix III).

It has been said that the Minster in Beaminster no longer existed at this time - that it had been destroyed in some way. This is clearly incorrect as St. Osmund lists, in the Register, churches that are part of the diocese and Beaminster is listed amongst these. This misunderstanding has arisen because no church is shown in Beaminster in the Domesday Book. This is because, in their terms of reference, the commissioners were instructed to include only those churches which paid tax to the Crown before the Norman Conquest. In the Exeter edition of the Domesday Book, for example, no churches are shown at Sherborne, Yetminster or Netherbury, although we know that churches existed in all those places. On the contrary churches are shown at Abbotsbury, that paid tax on 21 hides, Milton Abbas, 29 hides and Cerne, 22 hides.

The Register of St. Osmund opens with the Consuetudinary (i.e the Usage). This not only specified a liturgy to be used in all the churches and minsters, including Beaminster, but gave instructions on the behaviour of persons during worship. One example is instruction as to the manner one should leave one's seat if it was necessary to go out during the service. Some of these procedures are still traditional in the Church today. There were offices in detail for Festivals and Holy Days. A feature of these were the elaborate processions. All this was conducted in a simpler form in the local churches and minsters. These processions fulfilled a function for an illiterate population that stained glass windows did for a later time. They were a teaching aid for fundamentals of the Christian faith. A complete calendar of festivals was observed which included the Feast of the Holy Trinity which was not adopted for the Church of Rome until the 14th century. The Sarum usage began to have a much wider use. It was being used in Ireland in 1172 and in Lichfield in 1188. It has been said that of the churchmen of the 11th century no one was better known or esteemed than St Osmund. The Register also specified the duties and rights of the officials of the cathedral and other members of the cathedral body. In addition it laid down certain fees that were to be paid by the minsters to the diocese. These included fees for each high altar and also for side altars, which suggests that the minsters were perhaps larger than is sometimes supposed.

In addition to Benedictine priests there were also non-monastic clergy especially in the manorial churches. Problems with the clergy continued. The Bishop of Sarum was excommunicated in 1170. A circular letter to all clergy reads as follows:

STATUTUM DE CUSTODIA SIGILLORUM A.D 1214.

Preterea clerici singuli et universi in ecclesia mutua studeant evitare colloquia cum foeminabus de quibus possit suspicio oriri, quin pro talibus non modicum possit ecclesiae generari scandulum et detrimentum. Comestiones etiam et potationes cum hujusmodi mulieribus in ecclesia sub anathematis interminatione prohibentur.

Which translates:

(STATUTE OF THE KEEPER OF THE SEALS A.D. 1214.

Further, let each and every vicar in our churches be diligent to avoid converse with females which can give rise to suspicion, which when of an immoderate nature may generate scandal and harm for the churches. Also gluttons and drinkers and the sort that have a fondness for women are forbidden in the churches under penalty of perpetual excommunication.).

The Norman Church

In the 12th century the Benedictines decided to build a new church in Beaminster. There were apparently three reasons for this decision. First the population had grown in size. Secondly the area was now wealthier, having recovered from big payments such as Danegeld earlier and the depredations of the bishops and the crown. Thirdly the Benedictines had a new view of liturgy and the use of the church. From the 10th century onwards a great cultural stream flowed from Fleury on the Loire into England carrying the theological and liturgical heritage of the Carolingian renaissance. This included the form of usage known as the Carolingian Miniscule and a wave of devotion to the Blessed Virgin Mary. This was manifest in church dedications, the increased importance of the Feast of the Annunciation and the reckoning of the start of the year from Lady Day (March 25th). Fourthly the Benedictines followed their rule of life "Laborare est Orare" (To work is to pray) and so were prepared to do a lot of the work themselves with the help of travelling craftsmen for specialist items.

Thus a new church was built in Beaminster dedicated to St. Mary of the Annunciation and most probably dedicated on Lady Day. The Saxon Minster was not demolished but converted to other uses as recorded in the Sarum Registers (q.v. The Mansion House). The new Norman church was cruciform in shape, consisting of chancel, nave and two transepts, north and south. There was a central tower which spanned the entrance to the chancel. The building was placed more centrally in the graveyard, Saxon superstitions no longer being fashionable. We do not know the date of completion of this church but there are three existing artefacts by which we can arrive at an approximate date.

The most important of these is the font and it must have been in place by the time the church was dedicated. The present font is the original. It was thrown out in the 'restoration' of 1862 / 63 and replaced by a Victorian font. This was donated by a Miss C. Keddle at the cost of £40. However in 1927 the Norman font was discovered in George Symes builder's yard in what is now 24a Fleet Street. The square block holding the bowl and the base were intact but the central portion - the stem and supporting pillars - was damaged. These were copied by Joseph Keech and Sons, monumental masons at their premises in Church street and Hogshill Street, using a different stone, so that the restoration is clearly visible. The font was replaced in the church, the Victorian font removed to the Holy Trinity church and the Holy Trinity font moved to Stoke Water House.. The square block of this font has some engraved arcading on one side. This shows that the font cannot be later than the third quarter of the twelfth century because after that time the arcading extended around the whole font and became more elaborate. Further the four supporting pillars around the central stem stand directly on the base. In the latter part of the 12th century such pillars were given small pedestals of their own. This 12th century font was the work of a travelling craftsmen which was common at the time. The font in the church at Loders, of the same date, was made by the same man. Craftsmen made their own tools during their apprenticeship so that the marks made by each tool were as unique as fingerprints. The tool marks at Loders appear to be identical with those on the Beaminster font.

The Parish chest also supports the date for the Norman church. This chest is not later than the early part of the 13th century. Professor Nicholaus Pevsner researched the criteria for dating such chests and these are easily applied to the Beaminster chest. The earliest chests were monoxylons (i.e. hollowed out from a single tree trunk) but by the 12th century they were being made from planks of wood, with no joints, but held together with hand-made wrought iron brackets. This is exactly what we have in Beaminster. At first the chests had thicker end pieces than side pieces said to be following the tradition of the monoxylons. A little later all the planks were of the same thickness such as the St

Mary's chest. The hand made hinges involve intricate scroll work on the lid. Later in the 13th century the scroll work disappeared and the lids had carved decoration (except for certain chests known as 'Spanish' chests). These chests had drop handles and were usually painted on the inside. This is clearly not the case with the Beaminster chest. Further this chest is made of elm whereas later chests were made of oak and the planks were jointed together. The writer has checked this on two chests, later than the Beaminster chest, in the Palace of the Popes at Avignon. These have joints and carved lids. The Beaminster locks are also intricate and the hand-made keys are also of interest. Each of the two locks has its own key and each key is the mirror image of the other. This meant that if two monks, who had charge of the valuables and records, had a key each then the chest could only be opened when both were present. One of the feet of the chest is slightly damaged. This was caused by damp in earlier times. Through Norman and Mediaeval times there was no seating in the church except some benches around the walls for the elderly and infirm. Hence the expression "backs to the wall". The rest of the floor was covered with straw, which got damp, causing damage to the feet of the furniture. Each autumn, with some ceremony, the straw was taken out into the churchyard and burnt. Then wagons arrived with the new straw.

In the south-east corner of the present south aisle is an early piscina for washing the vessels from the altar. This was, in the Norman church, the south transept. Here was the altar to St Mary and St Juthware who will be considered later. The piscina is Early English. trefoil arched with pyramidal hood. By the end of this period in mid 13th century the ornamentation had become more lavish. This points to this piscina being of the latter part of the 12th century. There is a similar piscina in the church at Winterborne Abbas which is dated 1320 and is much more developed. The end wall here contains Norman work including typical dog-tooth ornamentation. This stone was probably re-used later when the rood loft steps were built. However it is unlikely that the stone was brought from elsewhere as has been suggested. At the time of its use there would have been piles of Norman stone from demolishing the Norman church and later its central tower.

It is possible that some relic of St. Juthware was kept here - that being quite a usual practice and the more likely since the Benedictines came from Sherborne, where St Juthware was revered. This then became a place of pilgrimage. Numbers of pilgrims, probably on their way to Sherborne, continued to arrive certainly through to the 16th century. There are accounts of miraculous healings at this altar. One pilgrim Sir John Gone died whilst on his pilgrimage here in 1497 and is buried in the south aisle. A purple marble altar was erected against the south wall to his memory.

Hutchins in his Dorset History following the manuscript collection of J.B. Russell, and quoted by Hine, states that he may have been a Knight of Malta. This is impossible since the Knights of St John of Jerusalem did not go to Malta until 1530 when they had been expelled from Rhodes by the Turks. Nevertheless he may well have been a Knight of St John of Jerusalem. The inscription on his ledger stone, not easy to decipher, reads "Pray for the soule of Sir John Gone whose body lyeth berid under this tombe on whose soule Jesus have mercy. A Paternoster et Ave".

During this time the Mort House was also built as a separate building not connected to the church. Until recently this was thought to be 16th century but recent work has revealed the earlier date as will be seen.

St. Juthware

St Juthware, a martyr, lived with her husband in the village of Halstock. Her story is part history and part legend. Surprise has sometimes been expressed that her name is Celtic and various

Illumination from the St. Juthware Mass in the Sherborne missal c.1400.

hypotheses have been constructed on this fact. There is, in reality nothing unusual about this. The British with their Celtic names were not all driven to the West by the Roman and later Saxon invaders. Most intermingled with the new arrivals and intermarried. Juthware's husband was probably Saxon. Juthware's name in Anglo-Saxon was Judewara. Juthware, herself, was the daughter of a nobleman. After the death of her mother Juthware helped the pilgrims passing through Halstock on their way to Sherborne. Her jealous stepmother goaded her son to kill Juthware. Whereupon he lopped off her head with a sword. Legend now takes over and it was said that she picked up her head, walked into the church and fell down. First that was physically impossible and secondly there was no church in Halstock at the time. The manorial churches in the Beaminster area did not arise until much later. She was buried in Halstock and the Church declared her a martyr. We know nothing of what happened to her husband or his mother.

Bishop Alfwold (1045 - 1058) had a more imposing shrine built for St. Wulfsige and the remains of St. Juthware removed to the cathedral church at Sherborne, now the Abbey. Her tomb was placed alongside that of St Wulfsige. The Sherborne missal, c.1400, contains a mass for St. Juthware's day (July 13th) with marginal illumination illustrating her martyrdom. Judith Hill Halstock is named after her.

The Peculiar

The unsatisfactory behaviour of priests and bishops continued into the 13th century despite the staffing by Benedictines. Further the bishops were becoming too powerful with their landed estates. The Pope, therefore, concerned with these reports, decided to make Beaminster a Papal Peculiar, that is a church independent and not answerable to the bishop. The bishop at the time was Bishop Simon of Ghent (1297 - 1315). From that time on the Churchwardens Scripts (i.e. their annual reports) were sent to the Dean of Salisbury and not to the bishop. This was not because of his office as Dean but because he was at that time Patron of the living. This procedure then continued through the ages. Although Beaminster was transferred to the Diocese of Bristol in 1542 and not restored to Salisbury until 1836. The earliest of these scripts still extant is dated 1585. This status was overlooked at the Reformation and was not corrected until Acts 6 & 7 of William IV and finally abolished by the Ecclesiastical Commissioners Acts of 1836 and 1850.

But on December 16th 1298 Bishop Simon of Gandavo, as he was known, wrote a letter to the church at Beaminster. On the face of it the letter looked like a complaint that the church had not been consecrated years after its construction. The idea that the ministers would have continued to use the church when they could have consecrated it seems extraordinary. However on August 23rd 1303 he wrote a second letter. The facts seem to be that the Bishop received a fee for every church consecrated and his letter is really saying that he has not had his fee and is not recognizing any church until he has. In fact in his second letter he is threatening to come down and collect his money for himself. There is no record of this church being consecrated in response to the letters and there seems little doubt that it already was, but, being now a Papal Peculiar, no fee was going to be paid to a bishop who no longer had any jurisdiction over Beaminster.

Endowment of the Chantry

By an Act, the 8th of Henry IV, in 1407, "it was found not to Be to the King's damage if he granted license to Robt Grey of Bemystre to give 2 messuages (dwellings), 40 acres of arable, 12 acres of meadow and ten acres of wood with appurtenances in Mortmain, to maintain a chaplain and celebrate daily at the altar of the Blessed Mary and St. Juthware". So this chantry was endowed with land presumably in Chantry farm. The rectors of this chantry were quite independent of the vicars of the church. A 'capital mansion' was 'built for their accommodation' almost certainly using the disused Saxon Minster site which is now the site of the Strode room.

The Present Church

By the beginning of the fifteenth century the church was considered to be too small for the population. During the years 1440 - 1460 the Norman church was gradually demolished and replaced with a new building. Where possible the Norman foundations were still used. In the process the transepts were extended into the north and south aisles. The central tower was left in place but new pillars and arches were built to support the nave roof. These, of early fifteenth century pattern had the typical running vine angular capitals, wide fluting and are well preserved in the church today. These formed an arcade on each side of the nave. The width of the arches was increased as one moved from east to west. This was a well known device to enhance the perspective. The extension of the south aisle now connected the Mort House to the church. Parts of the earlier walls were incorporated. These were in the eastern end of the north aisle and the eastern end of the south aisle. On the outside of the east wall of the south aisle is some Norman work. It has been suggested that this stone was brought from elsewhere. This is very unlikely since much Norman stone was lying around as demolition took place and no doubt the craftsmen used some of this. The altar dedicated to St Mary and St Juthware was retained and the accompanying piscina. The larger church created a problem in the conduct of services. It was considered essential that everyone should see the Elevation of the Host during the mass at the high altar. This was not possible in larger churches so it was decreed that it was in order if those unable to see could see someone who could. To assist this hagioscopes (or squints) were constructed providing a view from the side aisles to the high altar. The one in the south aisle is still in existence but that in the north aisle has been removed by later building.

A rood loft was also constructed with stone stairs leading to it from the front of the south aisle. This was a narrow gallery extending across the chancel arch. The rood (cross) always bore a figure of the crucified Christ. Lights were kept burning before the rood, especially during festivals. By order of the Council of Edward VI in 1547 the rood crosses were removed. However they were restored during the reign of Queen Mary but finally removed by an order of Queen Elizabeth I in 1560. All that remains now in St Mary's church are the rood loft stairs.

The Hillary Aisle

The two parts of St Mary's Church that have seen the most changes over the centuries are the Hillary Chapel and the south aisle. The earlier years of the Hillary Chapel, originally known as the Hillary aisle, are well recorded in Hutchins, Hine and by Marie Eedle. It is thought to have been built in 1505 by John Hillary of Meerhay; that is some 50 to 60 years after the building of the chancel and the structure of the north window supports that date. It may have been built as a chantry. The report of the Commission of 1548/9 following the Act of Edward VI abolishing chantries mentions only the Walter Grey chantry in Beaminster church but cites three lots of chantry land. Although the rent is the same, £3 4s 6d, these are different pieces of farm land and it is possible that one of them refers to the Hillary aisle but there is no firm evidence. The altar was originally under the east window. Shelves for candles and for images of saints are still there. When this altar was removed is unknown but it was probably during the reign of Edward VI. The piscina, for washing the vessels from this altar, in the south-east corner of this chapel is not without interest, although it is now blocked off and serves as a sort of book cupboard. It is generally thought that this was a combined piscina and squint to the high altar. That is unusual but other examples are known elsewhere in the country. The east window of the chapel was of stained glass in mediaeval times. All that remains are small pieces of glass in the upper part of the window. These are crystallized with age as can be clearly seen. The chapel was 'beautified' by Mary Mills of Meerhay in 1767 and repaired and newly covered with lead by William Clark of Beaminster in 1794. However the parclose screen separating it from the chancel was removed by the vote of the Vestry in 1825.

The Hillary family and their successors certainly owned the chapel and it remained unappropriated until 1848. Until that year the Sunday school children had used the Hillary chapel but Mary Clarke, the owner of the chapel, (it being an endowed chantry) requested that the children be removed on the grounds that this was not the use for which the chapel had been provided. This was obeyed on 13th of April 1852 In 1898 Mrs. Cox provided a new roof for the Hillary chapel at the cost of £190. The new roof was of oak and an exact copy of the earlier one, including the carved bosses.

Many members of the Hillary family and later owners of Lower Meerhay are buried beneath the chapel. Their memorial brasses are placed on the north wall of the chapel. That to Ann, wife of Henry Hillary, who died 16.2.1653 carries the following verse:

Tis not because this woman's virtue dy's
That the brass tells us here Ann Hillary ly's
Her name's long liv'd - she is in this commended
The poore cry out they'r Hillary term is ended.

The reference is, of course, to the Hilary Law and University term in the first quarter of the year. Another plate shows that some Beaminster people were quite long lived by eighteenth century standards: Wm Mills 1760, aged 82 years, and his wife 1771, aged 95 years.

Planning a new Tower

Towards the end of the 15th century the central Norman tower was removed and four pillars and arches were built to support the roof in its place. These have narrower fluting and smoothly curved moulding of the capitals which dates them at the end of the 15th century. They are part of the present church. There is, however, a puzzle over these pillars which remains unsolved. They are all of different heights. This would be understandable if those on the south side differed from those on the north, since the original Norman transepts were of different heights, but each of the four is of a different height and the curtain wall above has been modified to keep the nave roof level. These pillars stand on substantial blocks of limestone below floor level. However, in the early 1980's, when the Victorian wooden floor was being replaced it was discovered that the base block of the second pillar from the chancel on the south side had completely disintegrated leaving an air gap. The whole of the weighty pillar was, in fact, hanging from the top and could have collapsed at any moment! Some concrete was rushed in as an emergency repair.

The two stone sedillas in the chancel were left in position and the chancel entrance was replaced with a 2-centred arch of Ham stone, its soffit with double panels divided into tiers. Two skylights were made in the chancel roof. However the planners faced a difficult problem. They intended to build a square tower in the perpendicular style. Such towers had two buttresses on each face and a turret stair at one corner. If you now abut such a tower against the west wall of a church you have a problem with the two buttresses on the east face. Several solutions have been tried for this problem. For example at Sydling the buttresses were brought down to ground level outside the nave which was restricting. Alternatively they were cut off and corbelled above the roof as at Affpuddle. Thus extra weight was added to the tower with no extra support. The tower builders of Beaminster devised a better solution. They decided to replace the west wall of the nave with a Ham stone panelled arch similar to the chancel arch. The common wall between mort house and tower was also replaced with an arch. The east wall of the mort house remained as a wall with a door in it. The present arch in this wall of the mort house is of later date. It should be noted that it is not panelled like the other arches. This meant that two solid pieces of masonry were formed where the responses of these arches met the arches of the last bay of the nave. The two buttresses were to be brought down on these. However another problem now arose. The width of the nave was not sufficient to contain the east wall of the tower and the turret stair. The tower, therefore, was located some eighteen inches north of the central line of the nave, which allowed the turret stair to be just outside the church wall.

In due course the tower was constructed to this design. Today, standing in the nave, it can be seen that the western arch has a curtain wall of eighteen inches on its south side but none on its north side. Further more it can be seen that the apices of the western arch and the nave roof do not coincide.

The Tower

The tower was built as planned about the year 1500 in the reign of Henry VII. Any earlier and Beaminster might have found itself facing a heavy tax had it not been for the fact that John Morton, Archbishop of Canterbury and Chancellor, who was a native of Bere Regis died that year. It was his practice to levy such charges under what was known as 'Morton's Fork'. The will of one William Mason, dated 1504, requests that he be buried 'under the new tower' so the tower must have been complete, or nearly so, at that time. Later we read that his sister was also buried there and possibly other members of his family.

The tower is properly defined as square perpendicular, crenellated with crocketted pinnacles. Knowledgeable writers down the ages have described it as a gem of the West Country, which indeed it is. The church is listed as one of 'The Thousand Best Churches'. Prof. Nicholaus Pevsner declared it "One of the most ornate of Dorset Towers". English Heritage in its description states: "The higher stair turret is a stockade of pinnacles - they even grow out of the angles of the tower - this spectacular tower is an unrestrained display of sculpture".

The builders marked the tower as an outstanding building in a traditional way. Between the tower plinth and the first stage, instead of the usual string stones, they placed a row of quatrefoils. Similarly between the first and second stages they placed a row of paterae as the string. Both these ornamentations remain in very good condition, particularly the paterae. Other examples of this quality marking can be seen on the Magdalen Tower in Oxford, on several Somerset towers, and on the Cerne Abbas church. This was often done after the tower was completed.

The crockets are the bunches of curled leaves and flowers which sprout in stone from the sides of the pinnacles. They are even said to have been used as footholds by workmen in former times - no safety at work regulations then! It is held by some that the pinnacles are a Victorian addition. This is totally incorrect and arises from three different prints of drawings by Abel Bugler in the middle of the 19th century. These were published in 'The Gentleman's Magazine'. One of these is published in Marie Eedle's 'History of Beaminster'. A casual inspection seems to show the tower without pinnacles. Closer examination reveals that all the side pinnacles are in place and the lower plinths and springer stones on which the pinnacles rest are present at the top of the tower. In fact these drawings were made when the upper pinnacles had been removed for restoration. The pinnacles were placed on the tower at its building.

The pinnacles were not of original design but inspired by gothic examples such as those at Reims (c.1240 AD) and Notre Dame in Paris (c.1340). Early examples in England can be seen at Beverley Minster (c.1350).

In 1662 the weathercock was added to the tower. This was intended we are told to remind the people of Peter's denial of Christ. The churchwardens accounts read:

1662 pd Hugh Gale settinge upp of the weathercock 6d.

Payd ye Clarke for helpinge up of ye weathercock 6d.

A Saga of Pinnacles

The noted pinnacles of the Beaminster tower have certainly suffered the slings and arrows of fortune down the Ages. Originally there were 38 free standing pinnacles on the tower. Three more were added later. This does not include the six small pinnacles shown embedded in the masonry of the west face.

In the mid seventeenth century, Cromwellian times, some of the mob got onto the top of the tower and damaged some of the pinnacles, which up to then seemed not to have caused many problems. Following this there are two entries in the churchwardens accounts: "1667 Pd Hugh Sugar for 5 clamps for ye pinnacles at the toope of ye towre 2/6d" and "1667 Henry Peach for stownes and 2 days labor about the pinicles of the towre & Lyme 00-4s-00d." The next record we have of restoration is in 1861 but it seems that as far as the tower was concerned this was confined to some refurbishing. However by 1876 when Canon Alfred Codd was Vicar and David Symes and Richard Swatridge were Churchwardens the Vestry Meeting was expressing some concern about the tower. On the 19th of May it was decided to obtain estimates of the cost. The following week the estimates were ready totalling £950 including 13 pinnacles and faces and angles of the tower £150, clustered pinnacles and parapet £160 and scaffolding £200. There was much discussion and it was thought that the whole work could be done for £350 and a public notice to that effect was put out on 2nd of June. No one was engaged to do the work at that price and eventually something had to be done and on April 17th 1877 it was decided to go ahead. Mr William White of 30a Wimpole St, London was the architect and Mr Trask of Norton-sub-Hamden was the contractor. On April 21st the pinnacles were removed at a cost of £39-1 1s. Work went on throughout the summer and on October 9th Mr Trask finished and presented his bill for £875 plus £4-15s for an additional pinnacle. At this point legend takes over.

The usual story is that a Thanksgiving for the restoration was held on Sunday Oct 14th when a storm came up and blew all the pinnacles down. That would have been strange indeed since the storm actually occurred on the following Wednesday the 18th. A Thanksgiving had been arranged for November but that was postponed. The top of the tower was damaged. Telegrams to London brought Mr White's man, Mr Faulkener, two days later and the following week Mr White himself. His report shows that two pinnacles were blown down, the highest ones on the NW and SW corners. In falling one had damaged the top of another. No other damage had been done but it was thought that the small pinnacles on the turret might have been loosened. Mr White promptly blamed the contractor and in a letter on Nov 2nd he refused to agree that Mr Trask be paid.

A storm of another kind now broke. Mr White complained that the mortar and cement used was of inferior quality and that the bedding cement in one case was only 1/16th inch thick, still soft enough to be scraped out with a pocket knife after three months setting. He declared that the slate dowels that hold the pinnacles together should be 2" square and inserted 5" into the stonework.

These dowels should be, he said, of Delabole slate from North Wales whereas Wiveliscombe slate had been used and that Aberthaw lime should have been used in the mortar. Mr Trask rejected these complaints. Eventually Mr Trask was not only paid but engaged for further work on the tower. We frequently read in Canon Codd's letters of the wagon being sent to Crewkerne station to collect materials. A contemporary billhead shows that Mr White was also running a separate business from Wimpole street supplying materials for the restoration of churches and did in fact supply materials to Beaminster. On November 30th Mr White sent details of a method to speed up the setting of mortar. Now we should consider that this reduced the strength of the structure.

By early December 1877 the parishioners were querying whether it was safe to ring the bells and were assured by the architect that it was. In a paper on Dec. 17th Mr White sets out test pulls for the pinnacles. Large pinnacles were to withstand 260 lbs applied by a horizontal cord to the mid-point and smaller pinnacles 215-200 lbs. His calculations, of course, made no allowance for wind drag on the tower or turbulence since the science of Aerodynamics was still in the future. Neither did he consider the oscillation common to all towers and masts although this was well known in 1877. Mr White learned from the Royal- Meteorological Society (yes it had existed since 1866) that the strongest gales had a force less than he had supposed, so, two days later, he reduced the test weights to 200-210 lbs and 175-180 lbs respectively. Modern hindsight might consider that Mr White thus destroyed any safety margin that he might have had. Fortunately the calculations were sufficiently inaccurate to allow for that and no great disaster followed.

On June 18th 1878, the work on the tower being completed and other earlier work inside the body of the church, a Thanksgiving Festival was held. Venerable Archdeacon Lear preached. The text was "There was a certain householder" from Matt. 21 v 33. The preacher pointed out how every part of the church had its own special meaning and becomes, thus, a spiritual teacher. St Mary's was in triple form -

"Three solemn parts together twine
 In harmony's mysterious line.
 Three solemn aisles approach the shrine
 - yet all are one".

The church is thus a symbol of the Trinity.

The collection produced £25 - 10s for the tower fund. Parish choirs took part and afterwards had a substantial tea with the clergy at the White Hart. In the evening a successful concert by the Beaminster Musical society raised a further £12 for the Tower Fund.

However 1878 did not see the end of the saga of the pinnacles. In 1883 one pinnacle was replaced by Harry Hems of Exeter at a cost of £20. By 1902 there was further trouble and Messrs C & A Hann secured some of the pinnacles. A letter from Mr Kitson in November 1903 shows that Alice Toleman had collected £67-14s for repairs. Subscriptions ranged from 2/6 to £2-10s. It is interesting to note that some of the same family names occur amongst contributors today. In 1911 a pinnacle fell from the east side and damaged the nave roof. This was repaired by A. Hann & Sons and with lead supplied by A & E Toleman. In July 1911 an inspection was made by Charles E. Ponting architect and diocesan surveyor. Four pinnacles were found to be cracked including the east central one again. Bands of ironstone in the stonework appeared to be the problem. More copper cramps were recommended to be let in and run with sulphur. Thus trouble was again stored up for the future since sulphur slowly produces sulphuric acid which gradually changes copper into soluble copper sulphate. Mr Ponting did however note the vibration arising from the natural elasticity of the tower. Cost of repair was estimated at £61-10s if done from a sling platform or £40 more if done from scaffolding. A.V. Pine and J.L. Kitson, churchwardens, noted repairs were completed by Jan. 1912. In 1927 there was further trouble. The central pinnacle at the top of the east face of the tower fell through the roof of the church and smashed on the floor inside. Fortunately no one was in the church at the time and in 1987 the central east pinnacle was removed before it could fall on the roof once again and brought down into the church. Following this it was decided to carry out a complete inspection of the tower. Wessex Steeplejacks were engaged to carry out the task which they did on Monday October 31st 1988 under almost perfect conditions. The work was done entirely by harness and climbing tackle. Full notes were made, detailed drawings of all four faces of the tower and some 20 photographs of defects. They reported on the 8th of November.

The main structure of the tower was sound but there were most urgent and dangerous defects. These could be classified in several groups. First the lightning protection was virtually non-existent. Some years ago the flagstaff has been replaced with a fibre glass one. This had been lifted from the Vicarage lawn and installed on the top of the tower by using a helicopter. The lightning conductor had been removed to do this and had never been replaced. Only a tiny connection to the weather vane remained. Lightning conductors have to be inspected at regular intervals and are then date punched. Not a single date appeared on this conductor, the church was thus in breach of the law, had violated the regulations and the British Standards Code of Conduct for lightning protection of public buildings. In the event of accident there would have been no insurance cover whatever. Some years ago the Churchwardens would have been held responsible but now it was the collective responsibility of the whole P.C.C. It was imperative that the situation be rectified without delay.

Secondly at the top of the tower all the merlons of the parapet were layered and unsafe. Thirdly the pinnacles and faces of the tower revealed 29 pinnacles that needed attention but 3 were very dangerous and of these one at the S.W. corner was fractured in three places and most dangerous. A number of tie and cantilever stones were fractured or crumbling. Joints in the stair turret were displaced. There was spalling and fractures of a number of tie stones.

Normally the fractured blocks would be removed and new blocks would be carved to replace them. The cost, however, would be prohibitive. The steeplejacks suggested modern techniques for making the tower safe. They consisted of drilling and installing stainless steel or phosphor bronze dowels inside the stonework locked in place with modern resins. A small amount of new matching stone would be required. All the original quarries are closed but what is required could probably be obtained from Horn Park Quarries.

The total cost of the inspection including labour, travelling, fees, V.A.T and the cost of drawings and photographs was £419-46. The estimated total cost of all the required repairs was at least £20,000 with an extra £4,000 if the work was delayed for a year.

The Parochial Church Council agreed that the repair work should go ahead as soon as the necessary permission had been obtained and arrangements made. The lightning conductor system was renewed, the existing earth on the north side serviced and an additional earth constructed to the west of the tower. Collectors were taken to the top of the flagstaff and also to the top of the corner pinnacles.

By May 1989 sufficient funds were in hand to make a start on the tower. However the steeplejacks were unable to undertake the work until November 1989. Missing and badly fractured stones were replaced. Replacement stone from Horn Park proved totally unsuitable so material was obtained from Lympley Stoke. Salisbury Cathedral workshops were unable to help with any stone shaping or carving but Exeter Cathedral workshops volunteered to do this. All loose joints were raked out and repointed. The joints of the ashlar on the staircase turret were eased out and the displacement corrected. Any pinnacles found to be dangerously loose were taken down and rebuilt using stainless steel dowels minimum 250 mm in length by 10 mm in diameter set in the corners at least 50 mm from the front face where there was sufficient space. Where the bed was too small for this no 2 dowels were used. Particular attention was given to the western attached pinnacles on the north face, the central pinnacle of the west face, the southern pinnacle of the west face and the south-west pinnacle on the south face. The eastern central pinnacle was taken up from within the church and reinstated with stainless steel dowels. All loose sections of scale were removed and where there was sufficient body re-set with epoxy resin. Where there were open veins or incipient spalls these were secured with fine stainless steel pins. Similarly all figures, hood moulds, niches and string courses were examined and treated in the same way. The work was completed by 20.11.1989 and the final cost was £21,180-12.

In 2001 the tower was surveyed by English Heritage who considered that work should be carried out to clean and preserve the ancient statues and grotesques at an estimated cost of ½ million pounds. The whole tower was scaffolded for a period of six months. Essential repairs were carried out which included the pinning of loose stonework and inserting metal dowels through the pinnacles. The intent was not to restore the images but to preserve them in the original state and halt the weathering and deterioration that had occurred. Mortar was used for repointing and filling. Unfortunately cement had been used in the past and this was removed where possible and replaced with mortar but this was not possible in all cases and the cement had to be left for fear of damaging the stonework. All lichen, algae and other growth was cleaned from the figures. Following this they were given a ham-stone coloured lime wash. It is intended that this coating will take the weathering in future instead of the original stone and can easily be replaced when necessary. This coating is thin and does not alter the appearance of the images. The church architect Allan Harvey examined and recorded the age and state of all the stonework. Two archaeologists Allan Graham and Jerry Sansom studied and interpreted the figures and photographs were made for the record. The work was completed in March 2002.

The Tower Clock

The present clock is the second clock to be installed in the tower. The earliest known record of a clock is an entry in the churchwardens accounts for 1651 which reads: "ye Clarke was payd £1-17s-4d for keeping the bells and clocke and for other things". In 1675 a charge is entered "for making ye Clock and mending ye fourth bell clipper £6-10s-0d", in 1679 "pd ye Clarks Bill for keeping the Clock, Bells and Chimes £2". The year 1709 has this entry "Ralph Cloud received £10-11s-6d for his work about the bells and chimes". The present clock was installed in 1739; a brass plate attached is inscribed 'Ra Cloud the Maker 1739' and on the ironwork 'Wm Sanders - Hen Goold

Churchwardens'.

A Vestry meeting on 19th Nov. 1765 agreed to add a set of chimes, to be made by Thos. Bilbie Jnr. of Cullompton, to be playing by the 25th day of July next, with a penalty of 5/- for every week after that till the chimes be set to play. For thirteen years the chimes played two tunes alternately. However on April 8th 1780 the "dags" i.e. dogs or pins of the chime barrel were found to be worn and Charles Cloud and Henry Slade were asked to repair them. Instead they took the best pins from the two sets to make one good set. Since then the chimes have played one tune "Hanover" by Dr W. Croft in its original form every three hours.

In 1929 the clock was reconditioned by W.J. Ives the local clockmaker, most of the metal cutting being done by Francis Bugler, an agricultural engineer. Until 1968 the clock was driven by falling lead weights which were wound up daily by hand. In that year the clock was adapted to be driven electrically.

In July 1980 John G.M. Scott an inspector for the Central Council on Towers and Belfries and an expert on tower installations visited Beaminster. He prepared a report on the clock for the information of the Rector and the church members which is of such historic importance that it is reproduced here with full acknowledgement of John Scott's work and expertise:

Beaminster Church Clock

This is a fine clock movement of unusual interest for several reasons.

The frame is of wrought iron, with curved corner-posts of unusual design in that they curve inwards at the top. They are square in section, and the horizontal rails of the frame are riveted through them. The pivot bars which carry the three "trains" for the going, quarters and strike are curiously placed with the quarters and strike canted in at the top. One reason for this may he that three train clocks were in their early days in 1759; clocks which had quarter-chimes before this time more often had a "quarter-clock" in a separate frame, and in Devon we have only one clock, of 1725, made with three trains in one frame before this date. The well-known Dorset examples at 'Wimborne' and 'Sherborne' are both slightly later, I think. So the maker of the Beaminster clock may have had no examples to follow, and had to work out the best way of making his clock as he went along.

The wheels are all of iron except the brass escape-wheel which is a replacement, probably of 1929. The pendulum is also probably not the original one, as wooden pendulum rods came into fashion towards the end of the 18th century. The clock has been very ingeniously converted to electric power by fitting small electric motors to drive the fly arbors of the quarters and strike by chain and sprocket. The Quarter train in turn rewinds the driving weight of the going train. This has involved an absolute minimum of alteration in the clock; only the two flies have been removed, and most of the locking levers are still in place though no longer operational; the pieces removed are stored in the clock room, and it is to be hoped that they will remain so. Many clocks which are converted to electric power by professional turret clock firms are so mutilated in the process that one wishes that they had been left alone, and Beaminster is a shining example of the right way to do this kind of work.

The clock has a small oval brass plate on its centre pivot bar inscribed:

"Ra:: Cloud the Maker"   1759

Another similar plate below it reads:

"Re made W.J Ives"   1929

Both are beautifully engraved. On the front corner posts at the frame are engraved the words:

"Wm . Sanders Men. Goold Ch. Wardens"

There is no dial, nor ever has been. A great many church clocks of this period had no dial outside when they were first installed. The

Quarters chime: 1; 12: 123; 1254. Sherborne Abbey clock probably had the same quarters when it was installed, the "Westminster" quarters having been adopted for the present 19th century movement. The clock is beautiful order, and obviously well maintained. It ought to give years of service if it is as well looked after in the future.

The Chime Barrel

Chime barrels were much commoner in the 17th and 18th centuries than they are now, either manually operated to chime the bells before service (as at Colyton and Branscombe, where they chimed the bells in rounds) or weight-driven to play tunes at set intervals during the day, and set off by the clock. They work on the same principle as a musical-box, with levers connected to hammers on the bells pulled and released by pins on a revolving barrel.

This is a very fine example, and unlike most is signed and dated by its maker Thomas Bilbie of Cullompton, who installed it in 1767. Bilbie was a bell founder, but the family in Chewstoke were also clockmakers, as well as casting bells. The frame, which is of oak, is over 7 feet by 5, and the pin-barrel is 3 feet long and 4 feet in diameter. It is made of mahogany, and must be an early example of the use of that wood in this part of the country, if it is the original one. The winding-barrel is of elm. The barrel was wound by turning a crank on a large iron flywheel, which was geared down by two sets of cast-iron gear wheels and could be slipped, out of gear by sliding the idler wheel and pinion on their shaft.

At the other end of the frame is a small wrought-iron frame containing the second-wheel and fly. The uprights terminate in well-shaped scrolls, and carry a semi-circular plate inscribed with the maker's name, the churchwardens names and the date 1767 - two years after the casting of the bells. The original letting-off and locking gear is all still in place, and consists of a star-wheel which is locked by a lever and engages stop arms on the main barrel. The lever is released by being struck by a weighted arm which is lifted and released from the clock movement. This system, known as "kick-starting", was used for striking clacks in very early times, and persisted on chime barrels until the 19th century. There is an additional arm on this one to catch the falling weight and hold the chime barrel off.

According to the Church records, the barrel originally played two tunes. It now plays only one "Hanover" – in a form slightly different from the one now used.

Here again, it is very gratifying to find that the conversion to electric drive has been done so ingeniously and with so little mutilation of the chime-barrel. As with the clock, the drive is taken by way of a short chain to the fly arbor of the barrel, only the fly itself being removed.

John C. L. Scott
25th July 1980

The Bells

We now enter the stair turret of the tower by the external steps and door. These are a later addition. Originally the tower was entered from ground level inside the church through a door under the tower that was blocked up in the 'restoration' of 1862/3. The lower part of the stairs is still intact. In earlier times the bells were rung from the ringers' larte, as it was called, at ground level behind the western gallery, since removed.

The Inventory of 1552 shows only one bell, but by 1651 further bells and the clock had been added. As has been set out in the description of the clock the churchwardens accounts show various payments for the maintenance of the bells.

A Vestry held 16th May 1764 agreed to recast the bells, eight new bells being recast from the existing five. This was carried out by Thomas Bilbie and Son of Cullompton in a weaving shed adjoining the churchyard. The tenor bell was 37.25" high, 52.75" in diameter and weighed 25 cwt. The bells are inscribed "T. Bilbie Snr and T. Bilbie Jnr and/or Churchwardens Mr T. Harris and Mr J. Hearn". A vestry meeting on 19th Nov. 1765 agreed to build a new loft in the tower for bellringing and to add a set of new chimes.

Charles Hann repaired the tower in 1881 with pitch pine joists and new deal floors; the cost was £6 l2s, skilled men receiving 3s 8d a day, another man 3s and an apprentice 1s 6d. A & E foreman's bill for the fittings carried an advertisement, interestingly enough, for a patent new noiseless lawn mower! In 1903 W.B. Newman installed gas lighting in the belfry at a total cost of £5.

St Mary's bells had a considerable programme of ringing. The morning bell, probably the Angelus bell, was rung at 5 am until about 1860. The curfew bell sounded at 7 pm each evening until 1870. There was a bell for the start of trading in the market each week and for stopping; trading outside of these times was an offence. There are records of vestry meetings that dealt with offenders. There were similar rules for each of the two fairs, in May and September, which had been established by the charter of Edward I in 1284. This charter granted to William de Ewell and Thomas de Rupton, Canons of Salisbury Cathedral established Beaminster as a town. These bells were discontinued by Canon Codd. Fair days. Visitations, Vestry meetings. New Year's Eve, Nov 5th and Oak Apple day had regular peals. The keys of the belfry had always been kept by the vicar but on November 8th 1858 they were handed over to the leader of the bell ringers on condition that they rang only on days specified unless otherwise directed by the incumbent. They were no longer to be rung on Beaminster Fair Days. This was because there had been a disturbance at the September 20th fair. The Loyal and Thanksgiving peals included not only coronations and royal weddings but occasions such as the naval victory over the Dutch off Lowestoft in 1666, the relief of Ladysmith and the end of World Wars I and II. During World War II the bells were silenced in order to be used as an alarm. At 8 pm on Sept 7th 1940 General Headquarters, concerned about German activity across the channel issued the code word "Cromwell" to all Home Commands (this meant invasion imminent). However some Home Guard commanders, acting on their own initiative, had the bells rung to call out the Home Guard. This also happened in Beaminster. Rumours arose of parachute landings and U-boats approaching the coast. The Chiefs of staff had been unaware of the alarm and issued orders that bells were to be rung only when a group of parachutists had been seen and not because other bells had been heard or for any other reason. No mention of this was made in newspapers or in Parliament and it was looked upon as a useful rehearsal. However a minute from Prime Minister to C. in C. Home Forces on 30.11.40 reads "I have authorised the ringing of church bells on Christmas Day .... you will let me know what alternative methods of giving alarm you would propose to use on that day . . .".

Until recent times the Passing Bell was tolled in Beaminster - one stroke for each year of the deceased's life. This was preceded by nine strokes for a man, six for a woman and three for a child. Hence the saying "Nine tailors (tellers) make a man". The bell was also tolled for a corpse passing through the town. The shopkeepers then placed a single black shutter on the front of each shop window. Householders often drew their blinds until the cortege had passed. On Sunday March 31st 2002 a muffled peal was rung to mark the death of Queen Elizabeth the Queen Mother.

In the early eighteenth century Ringers Rules were placed in the belfry painted upon boards fixed to the south wall and later much defaced. The original in Old English characters reads:

Let awful silence trice proclaimed bee
Then praises given to ye Trinity
With love and honner pay unto ye King

Thus with a blessing rise ye cheerful ring.

- - - - - - - -

Hark how the chirping trible sings it clear
And capering Tom comes rolling in ye rear
Hold up on end, or stay! Come let us see
What laws are best to keep sobriety
So all consent and to this Law agree;
Who swears or curse, or in an angry mood
Quart Is or striks altho' he draws no blood
Who wears his hat, or spurs, or turns a Bell
Or by unskilful handling mars a peal
Let him pay sixpence - for each single crime
Twill make him causous 'gainst another time
But if the Secston's fault an hindrance bee
We crave from him a double penalty
Who dous our parson disrespect
Our Warden's orders any time negleget
Let him be held in foul disgrace
And ever after banished this place
Now round let's go with pleasure to ye ear
And pierce with cheerful sound ye yielding air
And when ye bells is cease, then let us sing
God save ye Church, God Bless ye King.

Anno Dom 1717.

We are told that the phrase "Hat or spurs" refers to visiting sight-seeing gentry who would sometimes enter the tower and have the audacity to try the bells.

In 1967 the wooden bell-frame was replaced with a steel frame and the bells turned and tuned by John Taylor of Loughborough. In 1972 the ringers themselves raised sufficient funds to install two more bells making a ring of ten. Mr Joe Barrett, Tower Captain was largely responsible for bringing about these improvements by his great energy and enthusiasm. It was under his direction the ringers raised most of the money for this; on his death his ashes were interred near the foot of the tower stairs.

The full list of bells was now:

Treble. Dia 28". 4 cwt 2 qr Inscribed "Given by the ringers 1972." John Taylor.

2nd. Dia 29". 5 cwt 2 qr "1972 John Taylor."

3rd. Dia 32". 6 cwt 2 qr "T. Bilbie Snr & T. Bilbie Jnr. Fecit 1765."

4th. Dia 32.5". 7 cwt 3 qr 7 lb. "Mr Thomas Harris & Mr John Hearn, churchwardens 1765. T.Bilbie fecit."

5th. Dia 34.25". 7 cwt 0 qr 16 lb "Mr Thomas Harris & Mr John Hearn, churchwardens 1765. T. Bilbie fecit."

6th. Dia 36.5". 8 cwt 0 qr 23 lb "Mr T. Harris, Mr J Hearn, churchwardens. 1765. T. Bilbie - Fecit."

7th. Dia 38.75". 9 cwt 1 qr 13 lb. "Thomas Bilbie & Sons. fecit 1765."

8th. Dia 41". 11 cwt 1qr 13 lb. "Mr John Hearn & Mr Thomas Harris, churchwardens. 1765. T. Bilbie fecit."

9th. Dia 45.5". 14 cwt 3 qr 12 lb. "Mr John Hearn & Mr Thomas Harris, churchwardens. 1765. T. Bilbie fecit."

Tenor. Dia 52.5". 22 cwt 1qr 27.5 lb. Note – D. Mr Thomas Harris & Mr John Hearn, churchwardens. 1765. "I to the church the living call and to the grave do summon all." Thomas Bilbie Snr & Thomas Bilbie Jnr., fecit."

In 1998 Mr J.C. Scott of the Towers and Belfries Committee of the Central Council of Church Bell-ringers inspected the tower and produced the following report:

Beaminster Church Tower & Bells

This splendid tower is over 100 feet high, built of stone, with clamp buttresses with a deep projection and an external polygonal stair-turret near the E end of the N. face. On ground level the walls appear to be about 4 feet thick, and the tower opens into the nave by a tall arched opening; there is a lower arched opening on the S side to a westward extension of the S aisle, and there is a door and a big five-light window on the W. A doorway to the stair from the inside has been blocked up, and access is now only by an outside door.

The ringing-room is in the second stage, which has a floor inserted to divide the ringing-room from the clock-room above it; windows on the N and E faces extend a little above this floor to light the clock-room slightly, and access to the clock-room is by a ladder from the ringing-room. Another ladder leads from the clock-room to the belfry, where the present floor is some feet below the original floor level. There is access to the belfry also from the stair.

The belfry is lit by two tall windows on each face, each window being divided by a horizontal band of masonry. The windows are all guarded against birds.

When the bells were rehung and augmented to ten, the new frame was built on a reinforced-concrete ring-beam at the level of the belfry offset. This was not made with the foundation-girders of the frame cast into it as is usually the case: the upper set of girders were bolted down to bolts cast into the beam, and the beam on the E and W faces was recessed to allow the lower girders to be bolted down also, thus obviating the very common problem of rusting where the steel meets the concrete. The foundation-girders are 15" x 6", all bolted together where they intersect and diamond-braced.

The bell frame is laid out with the 2,3,4,5, Tenor and Treble swinging E/W and the other four bells swinging N/S. This gives a total of about 50 cwt swinging E/W and about 45 cwt swinging N/S, which is a good balance with a tower which is stronger in the E/W axis. The bell frame has "A"-type frame-sides and is very well designed and built.

The only defects which I could find in the masonry internally were a small area of cracked stonework on the E side of the stair near the door which leads to the N aisle roof, and a crack above the N window of the ringing-room. Both of these cracks would be susceptible to thrust in the E/W axis, so I put an indicator across them and tested them with theTenor ringing. There was no trace of any movement in the cracks. Tower-sway was noticeable but no more than one would expect in a tower of this height; I have no way of measuring it, but on the basis of experience I would think that the Tenor by itself moves the tower less than 0.5 mm.

The whole bell installation is one of the best designed and laid-out that I have ever seen, and calculated to impose the very minimum of stress to the tower; it is a fitting monument to Joe Barrett who had so much to do with its planning and execution, and I would say that the ten bells in this frame and foundation must certainly do far less damage to the tower than the eight did in the earlier frame. It is likely that the crack in the N wall may have been caused by the stress imposed by that earlier frame; the damage in the stair is most likely due to the thrust of the N arcade and the wall above it, which meet the tower at this level. A strong gale would undoubtedly put far more stress on the tower that the bells in this installation.

In passing, I would like to commend the substitution of the usual stiff wires and cranks for the chime-hammers with flexible wires and pulleys; it makes the belfry so much easier and safer to work in.

John G. M. Scott.
December 12th 1989.

Bats & Jackdaws

For many generations the tower has been the home of Jackdaws who obtain their nesting material from Edmoncombe Copse. This often amounts to cwts! Many attempts have been made over the years to keep the birds out by netting the tower etc. These birds are quite intelligent and so far no one has succeeded. Even wire netting has failed. The birds work away at it until metal fatigue makes it give way.

Quite often, on a fine morning, they cluster on the east face of the tower so that they are warmed by the first rays of the rising sun and are then ready for the day's foraging. Jackdaws pair off for the whole of their relatively long life. There is no divorce amongst jackdaws.

The tower and body of the church is also the winter home of bats, principally pipistrelle. They leave in the spring and return at the end of August. Except that at times a few nursing mothers stay for the summer. They hibernate, not so much in the tower, but in the interstices of the nave roof and mort house which are probably warmer.

The Tower Images

The images on the tower have deteriorated during the early years of this century. The pollution produced by the Gas Works and by Cow and Gate Milk Factory played a considerable part, no doubt, in the erosion as did the smoking chimneys of every house in Beaminster.

One of the remarkable features of the tower are the carved springer stones of the pinnacles and label stops of the window mouldings. These take various forms. On the west face they are carved as cherubs holding open books probably representing the heavenly choir. Elsewhere, and particularly on the east face the carvings are of human heads and busts. Some of these may well represent patrons or dignitaries of the time and, perhaps the builders. In the centre of the east face a person is shown carrying a heavy hammer over his shoulder which supports this idea. Another depicts a man playing a bagpipe like wind instrument. Others show demons and mythological animals, although weathered now, are beautifully designed and carved so that their legs appear to be clasping the stonework. They are sometimes mistaken for gargoyles. There are, however, eight gothic gargoyles on the main body of the church. Most unusually one on the south side is in the form of a crocodile. Although to modern eyes it looks more like a pig, in mediaeval times few had actually seen a crocodile. Another less usual carving

Tower Images
Resurrection   Ascension

is the cherub with lute on the south face of the tower. The carvings on the west face are also notable.

Immediately above the west door a carving depicts the Nativity. The crowned Madonna is enthroned holding the infant Jesus. She is flanked on the south side by a representation of St George and the dragon. The dragon seems to have fared better in the weathering than

The Crucifixion

St George. Visitors often query the identity of the badly weathered figure to the north of the Virgin and Child. It was a bearded St James the Less. Richard Hine, writing in 1913, states that all the figures were in good condition, except St James which was beginning to crumble. St James the Less is said to have been killed with a Fuller's bat and is thus the patron saint of weavers. We know that this figure was placed on the tower circa 1503 and almost certainly before 1504. So this shows that the textile trade already existed in Beaminster at that date. Above the Nativity is depicted the Crucifixion. By the cross

Travellling Wool Salesman

are the figures of the Virgin and St. John. Finally there are four topmost panels. The two central panels represent the Resurrection to the north and the Ascension to the south. These panels, which are unusual on churches, but are found on some cathedrals and churches, in similar if not identical design. Christ is shown rising from the tomb and in the other panel the lower hem of Christ's robe is seen disappearing into the clouds whilst the people below gaze upwards. It is possible that these sculptures are the work of travelling craftsmen who worked from a limited range of designs but it is likely that they were carved elsewhere and bought by the tower builders to grace their work. These two panels are flanked by figures which apparently represent the industry in the town at the time and helped to finance the building. The one on the south side stands for the flax industry. He holds a fuller's bat in one hand and a fulling mill in the other which were essential implements of the trade. The other figure seems to be a backpacker who travelled the countryside on foot selling the worsted cloth made in the town. It is likely that in the 16th century all the figures were brightly coloured and made a dramatic display to face the processions that entered the church by the west door on festival occasions.

The western buttresses carry four figures in ornamental niches. The lower figure on the south side is the Virgin Mary and above her Anna her mother. On the north side we have St. Joseph and in the niche above the Archangel Gabriel.

These figures are clearly in keeping with the original dedication of the church to St Mary of the Annunciation. During the restoration of the 1880s a workman arrived at the church to restore the images. Leaving his tools and drawings of the images he went off to the vicarage to report his presence. When he returned his tools were intact but the drawings had disappeared and were never seen again.

Harry Hems of Exeter was commissioned to replace the figures on the north-west buttress in 1878. One of Harry Hems most important works was the Great Reredos of St Albans Abbey. The upper figure

Saint Bega

that he carved for Beaminster personated King Alfred. There is no evidence of any direct connection of King Alfred with the Saxon church in Beaminster, although he was very interested in all the Saxon churches. He came to the throne in A.D. 871 following the death of his elder brother. He was concerned with the welfare of the churches throughout his kingdom and he was familiar with this part of his territory. He remained in this part for some time to be within reach of Appledore where the Danes were attempting to found a settlement and he had to relieve the seige of Exeter in A.D. 877, again in 894, and to respond to continual Danish probing along the coast.. He was a man far ahead of his time in education and in cultural matters, Alfred corresponded with Elias III Patriarch of Jerusalem, was in Rome at the age of five and spent a year there later in life. A lot of his work for the Church and the schools was in the last four years of his life on which the Anglo-Saxon Chronicles are silent. He wrote a preface to the "Dialogues of Gregory", translated Gregory's "Pastoral care" and Bede's "Ecclesiastical History". His book "Blostman", part of which is based on the soliloquies of St Augustine, concludes with these words, "Therefore it seems to me a very foolish man, and a very wretched, who will not increase his understanding while he is in the world, and ever wish and long to reach that endless life where all shall be made clear". No direct connection with Beaminster, perhaps, but he is worthy of a place on our tower. The lower figure is St Bea or Bega. She carries the palm of sainthood in her left hand and in her right a model of a church as appropriate for the founder of minsters. She was, of course, the patron saint of the Saxon minster in Beaminster.

The Tower as Art

Church towers can be considered as art forms in themselves. Alex Clifton Taylor writing in English Parish Churches as Works of Art states: "There are I believe four essential requirements for a fine tower. The horizontal divisions must be subordinate to the vertical. There should be strong angle-buttresses for, in large towers, these are of great importance visually no less than structurally. The tower should get richer as the eye moves upwards, with the horizontal divisions becoming loftier. And, lastly, the summit should be reconciled with the sky, a vital point, for if the termination is too abrupt the eye will register an uncomfortable jolt, like a vehicle coming to a sudden halt."

The Beaminster tower clearly fits this prescription perfectly. It also gives one reason for having pinnacles.

The Netherbury Myth

About the year 1640 John Leland is thought to have visited Beaminster because in the book Leland's Itinerary in England and Wales 1535-1543, which was not written by Leland, we read:

"Bemistre is a praty market town in Dorsetshire, and usith much housbandry, and lyeth in one streat from north to south; and in nother from west to est.

Ther is a fair chapelle of ease in this town. Netherby is the paroch chirch to it: and Bemistre is a prebend to the chirch of Saresbyri."

Some people have taken this at face value and have talked of Netherbury being the mother church. Others more discerning have been puzzled by this. The next few lines read:

"Bemistre is but 4 miles from Crookeshorn, a market in Somersetshir by north from Bemistre. Shirburn is 6 miles toward the est from Bemistre".

There can be no such location as Sherborne is more than twelve miles from Crewkerne and even allowing for errors in estimating distance this would place Beaminster in Somerset. So the accuracy of what is stated becomes suspect. Further it states that Beaminster is a prebend and these were arranged by parishes and could not have been attached to a chapel of ease. Moreover Beaminster had a font which no chapel of ease had and also rectors saying masses at one or possibly two chantries. Further Beaminster was some two hundred years older that Netherbury which had arisen as a manorial church within the minster area. The foundations of the present church at Netherbury are 14th century.

This puzzle is explained if the foreword to the book by Thomas Kendrick is read and also the introduction by John Bale of Trinity College Cambridge. John Leland was very seriously mentally deranged. No real diagnosis is possible at this distance in time but he was certainly an extremely aggressive psychopath who suffered hallucinations and delusions. T.D. Kendrick, author of "British Antiquity" states that the slightest criticism of Leland turned him "immediately into an angry, irrational creature, gibbering with indignation". He had been a royal librarian but had been dismissed from his post because of his intolerable behaviour. He attacked anyone who doubted his story that King Brutus of Troy was the founder of the line of British kings. By 1544 he was declaring that the legend of King Arthur was fact, that various mythical Arthurian sites were genuine and that he has seen King Arthur's coffin at Glastonbury. On his reputed visit to Bridport he stated that they made excellent daggers believing them to be knives. The Bridport dagger is, of course, the hempen halter used by the hangman (silken when the murderer was a peer). In York Minster he defaced the inscriptions as they did not agree with his ideas. Although the Itinerary covers only eight years he disappeared from London and wandered about the country for eleven years. What he actually did and how he supported himself is unknown but when he returned he was penniless. His friends compiled the Itinerary in an attempt to raise money for him. He had kept no notes of his journeys so they had to rely on what he said. Edward VI granted stipends from three livings for his sustenance. He died in 1552. This is the basis for the mythical story that Netherbury was the mother church!

Although Beaminster and Netherbury were never one parish they did form a joint benefice on three occasions David of Stalbridge was temporarily joint vicar in the reign of Edward III. Again in 1405 Thomas Harrington was vicar of the joint benefice. During the whole of the Commonwealth from 1649 Beaminster was an entirely independent parish, the vicar being Joseph Crabb M.A., but on the death of Jerome Turner of Netherbury in 1655 he became vicar of both parishes. Thus a joint benefice arose again. In 1656 a commission considered the state of the parish. It records that tithes and dues belonging to Netherbury had for five or six years been separated from Beaminster and that separate ministers had been appointed to each parish. The people of Beaminster prayed that this be so continued. The commission recommended that the chapel of Mangerton, formerly a chapel belonging to Netherbury, be annexed to Beaminster. The plurality of the two parishes continued for in 1728 John Gifford and Robert Brodrepp brought an action in the Court of Exchequer against Peter Brice who is named as vicar of Beaminster and separately vicar of Netherbury. The plaintiffs claimed the modesses, or customary dues, were owing. The dues being 1s. for each milk cow, 1s. for each acre of meadow and 1s. for each hogshead of cider. In 1837 the inhabitants produced a Memorial asking for a complete separation of the parishes. It was 1849 before the final separation took place and the notorious Rev. Flood became vicar.

There are at least two other occasions when Beaminster was legally defined as a separate parish. The Commission of 1548-9 which dissolved the chantry, in folio 5 of their report, state "The Chauntrye of Beamyster in the pysshe Churche of Beamyster" which clearly establishes Beaminster as the parish church. In a later part of their report, Folio 6, one reads: "Decanatus de Brydporte. 56 Cantia in ecclia pochiali de Beamist Johes Myntern incumbens" (i.e. The Deanery of Bridport. Clause 56 in the parish church of Beaminster John Mintern incumbent).

The Mansion House

With the building of the Norman Church the former Minster building became redundant. However the chantry in the new south transept had its own rector to conduct the prayers there and to receive the pilgrims. The Salisbury registers show that some of the Rectors who lived there in succession were William Vale (1408), Walter Salke (1421), John Aleyn, John Napper (1429), John Comeland, Walter Grey (1526), John Ernley, William Page, Roger Eyars (1534). Their work was entirely independent of the rest of the church.

However in 1547 the chantries were abolished by an Act of Edward VI. A King's Commission was set up to visit and report on the chantries. It reported in 1549 in a mixture of Tudor English and Mediaeval Latin. In Folio 5 we read "The Chauntrye of Beamyster in the pysshe Churche of Beamyster vjli iijs iiijd whereof in Rents resolute ijd and so remayn vjli iijs iid". In other words £6 3s 4d was annually paid to the rector, at this time, John Minterne, 2d of this was deducted for the rent of the mansion leaving £6 3s 2d. The report goes on to say that there was one chalice 7oz in weight and certain ornaments to the value of 8s 4d. Folio 6 gives us more information. One cow belonged to the chantry valued at 7s. From the historical point of view, more importantly, it says "Decanatus de Bridporte Cantia in ecclia pochali de Beamist", which means that the chantry was in the parish church of Beaminster in the deanery of Bridport. This is further evidence that the story of St Mary's Beaminster being a chapel of ease of Netherbury is untrue.

It also shows that Rev. John Minterne had a further 12s deducted for tithe leaving him with £5 11s 2d a year. It is certified that no other preacher, grammar school, poor people or beadmen were supported by the chantry. A beadman was a man hired to pray for others - he 'told' his beads (his rosary). John Minterne was evicted and the Crown leased out the chantry lands and the chantry house. The leases were granted to Sir Michael Stanhope and John Bellow in 1549 as King's

Commissioners for services rendered in lieu of money. In the normal course of events the sequestered property would have been returned to the Church in 1660 at the Restoration. There are many other examples of this. The Toller Whelme estates, for example, which had provided the timber for the re-building of Beaminster after the fire of 1644, were returned to George Penne with additional compensation granted by Parliament.

This did not happen in Beaminster because of the conversion of the Mansion House into Almshouses. The usual story is that this was carried out by Sir John Strode, Lord of the Manor, who bought the site and built and endowed the almshouses in the year 1630. The truth seems to be very different.

(1) Sir John Strode was not Lord of the Manor of Beaminster. He has been described as Lord of the Manor of Parnham, but it is doubtful if Parnham had any manorial rights. Sir John Strode was Patron of the Living from 1608 but the Patron had only the Rights of Advowson which gave him some control of clergy appointments and their stipends etc. The Patron had no authority in dealing with church buildings.

(2) There is no record of his ownership of the site nor of his passing it to George Strode on his death. It has been said that the record of his acquisition must have perished in the fire of 1831 at the Bishop's palace and library in Bristol. This cannot be the case. He could not have bought, or obtained possession of the Mansion House site in any way because it was sequestered property. The Crown leased out the sequestered property as we have seen but did not sell it.

(3) The Mansion House site was in mortmain from the time of the original endowment of the chantry. The mediaeval law of mortmain was in force until relevantly recent times and ensured that such property could not be conveyed to an individual without a license from the Crown. It has been said that the absence of a license must have meant that John Strode already owned the property. The opposite of course is true. It must be concluded that John Strode did not own the site.

(4) The almshouses were not built as such. The Mansion House was already in use as accommodation and was merely converted to its new use.

(5) This conversion did not take place in 1630. That idea arises from the stone plaque on the wall of the building which states 'God's House. Sit Honos Trino Deo,1630'. That was probably placed there by the Oglanders at a later reconstruction. It is clear that the almshouses were already there in 1627 as Sir John Strode provided maintenance for the almshouse by Deed of Gift in that year. In this deed a charge is made on certain fields at Bilshay farm Bridport for this purpose. This can be seen in detail in the Charity Commissioners Report which follows. However there were already St Helen's Rents levied on these fields. A St Helen's Rent (sometimes known as a Modes) was an annual charge on land which the owner had to pay to a specified charity, usually a church. In the case of Bishay farm £6 a year had to be paid to Symondsbury Church. Sir John Strode exempted this £6 from his gift. But it appears that there may have been another St Helen's rent on the property that was included and thus diverted to Beaminster.

The money for converting the almshouse no doubt came from the rents being paid for other parts of the sequestered property. One obscure document suggests that a St Helen's Rent from Lower Wraxall may have contributed.

Lady Joan Turberville, daughter of Sir John Strode, by her will gave £50 to be invested for the almshouses (a not inconsiderable sum in those days). This sum never appeared in the accounts and the story was that it had been used to buy the almshouse garden.

There is further evidence that the sequestered properties were leased is given in a note from the Beaminster Manorial Court which shows the widow of Sir John Strode as being a leaseholder:

Sir John Strode referred to 'his' almshouses but this is without significance as he called a part of the church, which he had taken over, his.

at a court holden for this manor, 1649, the homagers presented that "Mrs Joan Strode, widow holdeth by lease the impropriate parsonage of Netherbury & Beaminster with a house called the chantrie, with orchard & garden, by estimation three yard, & that there are likewise two woods belonging to the said prebend, the one called Clark's Wood & the other called Lyme Wood, out of which — — — — hath formerly paid: And that the vicar of Netherbury & Beaminster paid to the lord of this manor fortie shillings per annum fortie shillings per acre in lieu of tyth hemp.

Extract from the reports of the Commissioners (Commonly known as Lord Brougham's Commission), appointed, in pursuance of various Acts of Parliament, to enquire concerning Charities in England and Wales, relating to the County of Dorset 1819 - 1857.

****

BEAMINSTER ALMSHOUSES

We could not discover, from any authentic document, the origin of this endowment; but it is stated in Hutchins's History of Dorset, that Sir John Strode, knt. By a deed of gift, executed by him in or about the year 1627, gave two - thirds of Bilshay Farm (subject to the payment, out of the whole farm, of 6£. per annum to the church of Symondsbury) for the support and maintenance of his almshouse in the parish of Beamlnster.

It appears from a manuscript book in the hand-writing of George Strode, Esq, the grandson of the donor, that the farm then consisted of a messuage or tenement, barn, stable, and certain closes of land, containing, by estimation:-

	A.	R.	P.
Of arable	20	0	0
Pasture and meadow	30	0	0
	50	0	0

The present description of that portion of Bllshay Farm which belongs (as to two-thirds) to this charity, is, by a survey made in 1735, as follows :-

	A.	R.	P.
House, orchard, barton, and garden	1	0	14
Barley Close, arable	8	1	9
Colley Close, ditto	7	1	4
Dawtery Close, ditto	9	1	20
Yonder Hanging Close, pasture	2	0	39
Plain Close, arable	2	1	4
Pond Close, pasture	2	1	19
Middle Hanging, ditto	2	3	6
Mead, meadow	3	1	31
Ditto, ditto	1	0	1
Moor, ditto	1	3	24
Ditto, ditto	1	3	26
	45	3	37

The remaining third part of this estate is now the property of Sir William Oglander, of Parnham, bart., the representative of the Strode family, who is also in possession of the two thirds belonging to the charity,, and has let the whole, together with other lands belonging to himself, to Thomas Hussey, of Bilshay, for the term of eight years, from the sixth of April 1833. The rent paid by Hussey ie 140£., of which 35£. is considered to be in respect of the two-thirds of Bilshay Farm belonging to the charity.

The garden attached to the almshouses is let to **Mr.** John Hamilton, of Beaminster, clothier, at the yearly rent of 1£. 10.

The account - books of this charity show that Sir William Oglander and his predecessors have not regarded the amount actually payable to the almshouse, but have always supplied what was necessary for the repairs of the building and the maintenance of its inmates, there being no other funds applicable to this purpose. The average amount paid yearly, for the last 10 years, for the maintenance of the alms people, has been about 56£. The repairs of Bilshay Farm, and of the almshouses, have always been borne by Sir W. Oglander and his predecessors, without making any demand for it upon this charity - fund, as also the charge for medical attendance.

The persons maintained, in the almshouse are six in number, either men or women, who receive each 1s. per week, meat, bread, fuel, shoes, stockings, coats, and cloaks.

The inmates are chosen, by Sir William Oglander, from distressed persons of a better class, who have not generally received parochial aid; and the supplies are apportioned among them at his discretion.

The ancient Bilshay Farm (being the 43A. 3R. 37P.) will in future be let at a distinct rent, in order that the sum actually payable to this charity may be clearly ascertained.

The following information was extracted from the general digest of Endowed Charities - the 14th report of the Charity Commissioners (Lord Robert Montague) 15th July 1868.

Area of garden and two - thirds of Bilshay Farm	43A. 3R 37P.
Real estate value and gross income	41£. 17s. 2p.
Total former income	36£. 10s. 2p.
Support of almshouses, their inmates and pensioners	35£. 17s. 2p.
Amount applied in Symondsbury	6£. 0s. 0p.

*******************End of the extract *******************

The inmates of the Almshouse were subject to strict rules. These included attendance at church service twice on Sundays, attendance at the Communion service at least twice a year. Although the women were provided with food and clothing conditions were actually rather primitive. All water, for example, had to be fetched from the Flatters Chute at the bottom of Duck Street (now called St Mary Well Street). The women were chosen on the grounds of supposed good character. However this did not always follow. In 1640 there is an account of a woman excluded from the almshouse. The record reads: "An Almswoman of God's House aged about seventy-five years, having lived there for eight years, was removed and displaced for not frequenting the church nor receiving Holy Communion twice a year and for being a blasphemous swearer, a night prigger and desolate liver."

The Sir William Oglander concerned, the son of the previous Sir William Oglander, died in 1852. He was succeeded by Sir Henry Oglander who had little interest in Beaminster or its almshouses, spending most of his time in the Isle of Wight. The income from Bilshay was insufficient by itself to maintain the building which gradually deteriorated. Sir Henry's widow continued in the ownership of Bilshay until her death in 1894. By that time the number of inmates had been reduced from six to five. In 1899 the Rev A.A. Leonard, vicar and Cpt. Thomas Russell became very concerned about the status of the almshouses and its finance including the story that the £50 had been used to buy the garden. They employed Messrs Farrer of 66 Lincoln Inn Fields London to take the matter up with the Charity Commission. The Commission replied on 21st of July 1899. Their reference is B71287. They had no definite information on the ownership of the building but stated that £50 had been spent on the purchase of the almshouse garden "was the merest surmise". They then appointed three trustees to manage the almshouse. In 1903 Bilshay was sold and the amount due to Beaminster invested. The number of inmates were then reduced from six to four. By 1914 only three people were living there each receiving 3s 3d per week, In the 1920s Stoke Water House, which had been the workhouse and tramp ward, began to take in a few elderly people and the almshouse continued to deteriorate. In 1950 it was refurbished as two flats, each with a bed-sitting room, kitchen and sanitary facilities.

The Inventory of Ancient and Historical Monuments In West Dorset, compiled in 1954 by the Royal Commission on Historical Monuments England, described the Almshouses as "range of tenements on the N.W. of the churchyard, are of one storey. They were founded by Sir John Strode for six persons but are of three tenements only." The front has two original stone windows and one original doorway with a four - centred head; above them runs a continuous label. A stone panel bears the inscription "God's house, sit honos trino Deo Anno Dom. 1630". There are three original windows at the back.

The almshouses, in the N.W. corner of the churchyard are partially hidden by a low wall erected at a later date. There can be but little doubt that the ancient Chantry House was in use as an almshouse before Sir John Strode, an influential parishioner, some 80 years after dispossession of Chantry Chapels, undertook his scheme of rehabilitation.

The almshouse accommodation, originally for six people, has been reduced from three sub-standard tenements to two more acceptable units of accommodation, presumably to banish a perennial bone of contention. For proof that the expedient failed, one need only consider the present plight of the structure - after the passage of a mere 80 years - and the answer is incontrovertible so far as almshouses are concerned. Urgent consideration must be given to the preservation of this historic fabric and not put aside to await tomorrow which so often never comes. The re-emergence of this ancient precinctual Chantry House as a Church Room, within the boundaries of the Parish Church, from which it was estranged about 1547 would fulfil an urgent need and the time is now opportune.

Then the Local Authority built the first of its sheltered accommodation for the elderly and the almshouse gradually became empty. On the 6th of September 1952 the Commissioners revised the trust and set up a new scheme with four trustees who were: Rev. A.W. Wheeler, vicar, Mr R. Leigh, solicitor, Mr W.A. Stiby, solicitor and Mr R. Travers, clerk to the Rural District Council. In 1960 following the introduction of the Charities Act the Commissioners placed the foundation in the care of the Beaminster Parochial Charities trustees. By 1970 it was derelict, vandalised and a thoroughly undesirable site next to the church. In 1975 the Charity Commissioners decided to act and offered the almshouses to the church for £8,000. The P.C.C. rejected this offer and the parish treasurer, Mr Jack Vincent M.B.E. of Shadrack Street pointed out that the church funds could not meet this price nor the subsequent cost of restoration. Furthermore he declared that the almshouses were church property anyway. Together with a retired architect Mr Norman Edwards of Woodswater Lane he entered into considerable correspondence with Mr H.K. Uvadia of the Charities Commission. Between them they put forward some of the evidence that has been given here. Mr Uvadia ignored this completely including the 1954 Inventory just quoted which clearly supported Mr Vincent's contention. This was not helped by the fact that the rest of the P.C.C. took the usual folk-lore story as true, quoting Hutchin's History of Dorset, which has been shown to be completely untrue. They offered no other evidence to support their view. Fear was being expressed that the building might be sold to a developer who could pull it down or convert it to some unacceptable purpose. Steps were taken in an effort to obtain a reduction in price. The price was reduced to £5,000 but the P.C.C. were still not prepared to meet this. It was decided therefore in 1975 to set up an appeal committee to raise funds so that the building could be purchased in trust for the people of Beaminster. There was, however, another point to be settled. Was the handing over to

Beaminster Charities legal or were the actions throughout of the Charity Commissioners a matter of mal-administration? The good offices of the local MP James Spicer (later Sir James) was sought in order to bring the matter to the Parliamentary Commissioner for Administration. This was placed before the Commissioner on 10th of August 1976 and he replied on the 27th of that month. His view was that the attitude of the P.C.C. had left no case for a claim of mal-administration and so he could not act.

The appeal continued and by 1977 £20,000 had been raised, the building renovated furnished and equipped with a modern kitchen and toilets. The Strode Room was opened by the Lord Lieutenant of the County. Over the fireplace hangs the coat of arms of Sir John Strode which is extraordinary because the person who committed most of his own money to the almshouse was Sir William Oglander. Should it be called the Strode Room at all? The folk-lore story persisted to the end. In the Bridport News the chairman of the appeal committee Mr Wilfred Buckingham declared "They were built by Sir John Strode, and his descendants would have undoubtedly been responsible for the general administration of the building. It was never in possession of the church at that time or since"!!

The history of the almshouses raises the question whether church government as now constituted is competent to care for our historic churches and ancient buildings. Perhaps the coming of English Heritage as watchdog will be their salvation.

The Mort House and School

It was long thought that the Mort House was a 16th century building since the walls and roof certainly are. However in 1992 part of the floor was taken up to make provision for future drainage. It was then found that the foundations are 13th century so that the Mort House was built at the time of the Norman Church. The west door, which had been blocked up for well over one hundred years, was unblocked to re-instate the door. The stone door frame proved to be of the 14th century. In the stone are two deep sockets which enabled a baulk of timber to be slid across to secure the door. Since this was on the inside there must also have been another door to permit exit. When the stonework of the walls was cleaned small traces of colour were found so there may have been wall paintings in earlier times. The name Mort House comes from the Latin 'domus mortuaria', the house of the dead. Before the end of the 17th century memorial stones were uncommon in churchyards and the same part of the churchyard was used again and again, as it had been for centuries. Any bones uncovered were deposited in the Mort House. When this practice ceased the mort house was often used as a chapel of rest for corpses awaiting burial. It is not known whether this was a one or two storey building at that time. However when the present tower was built at the beginning of the 16th century the Mort House was reconstructed. The north wall was replaced by an archway into the under tower space. From that time there were certainly two stories. The upper storey was entered by a staircase from the churchyard near the western end of the south aisle. This was still there in the 19th century as can be seen from the church plan of that time (see page 94). By the mid 17th century a school was being held in the upper room. Tradition has it that the school had existed from much earlier times. Entries in the Churchwardens Accounts read:

1651. Payd to the Joynner for boarding the window
att the west end of ye school 0-2-6.
1663. To Mr Collett for a planche and a raile to
make formes for the schoolhouse 0-50.
1713. Three guineas were paid for tyles for ye
schoolhouse.

The normal curriculum for such a school in those days was the three 'R's and Latin. Sometimes a little geometry was taught chiefly for its application in land surveying. The school was endowed under the will of Frances Tucker in 1685 with land and money for scholarships for "twentie of the poorest Boyes of the parish". She died a spinster and was buried in the church. The funeral accounts include 2 yards of black cloth to cover the pulpit (32 sh), 40 dozen cakes (40 sh), and wine cider and beer (£4.10.0). By the terms of the will the boys were committed to the charge of a schoolmaster, who was to be paid £20 a year and he had "to take care of their manners, to catechise them, to teach them to read, write and in some competent measure to cast an account. The school was to be managed and ordered soberly and piously in the fear of God and for the better advantage of the children". In 1734/35 the school moved to a building at Tower Hill with a house for the schoolmaster. In 1781 that house was burnt down and the daughter of William Pavy, the schoolmaster, was burnt to death. Her memorial stone in the churchyard bears the following:

> SACRED to ye remains of ye unfortunate Betty Daughter
> Of William and Ann Pavy Aged 23 years who fell a sacrifice in ye
> Dreadful Conflagration which happened in this Town on Saturday
> March ye 31 at 1781. This stone is erected by her brother William
> Pavy Apothecary in London.

After the school moved out the Mort House was used for Vestry meetings. During the Canon Codd 'Restoration' of 1861/3 the upper storey was removed and the lower storey became a vestry.

Some of the schoolmasters were:

Launcelotte Crabb	1634
William Coombe	1703
Joseph Harbin	1709
John Harbin	1711
Rev. Samuel Hood	1715

The latter was also Vicar of Thorncombe and father of the distinguished Admiral Sir Samuel Hood K.B. (1st Viscount Hood) and Sir Alexander Hood K.B. (1st Baron of Bridport).

Rev. John Guppy	1724
John Martin	1732
William Paviott	1757
James Ames	1779
Benjamin Ames	?
Richard Ames	?
William Whitelegg	1800
John Shapland	1832

An account of the further history of the school can be found in the Beaminster Area Team Handbook 1984 written by Mr R.C. Travers and published on the 700th Anniversary of the granting of the town's Market Charter.

Beaminster's Bishop

Whilst the school was still in the church one of its pupils was a notable son of Beaminster - Dr Thomas Spratt. The son of the Minister the Rev Thomas Spratt he was baptised, as recorded in the Parish Registers, on Sunday September 20th 1635. Born in Beaminster as he stated in his "Sermon before the Natives of Dorset" on 8th December 1692. As he later records in his autobiography he received the rudiments of his education at the little school by the churchyard side in Beaminster. (The entrance to the school was by the buttress at the south-west corner of the south aisle). This says something for the quality of education there at that time. At the age of 16 he matriculated and entered Wadham College Oxford, took the M.A. degree in 1657 and held a Fellowship from then until 1670. He was elected a Fellow of the Royal Society in 1663 and wrote a history of that body in 1667. He took the degree of Bachelor of Divinity and the Doctorate in 1669 when he became a Canon of Westminster. In 1676 he was chaplain to Charles II, in 1681 a Canon of Windsor, in 1683

Dean of Westminster and the next year Bishop of Rochester. He was well known as a poet, wit, preacher, lecturer, historian and man of letters with numerous publications. He wrote a history of the Rye House Plot but evaded the king's command to account the invasion of Monmouth. Dr Johnson described his books as "each having a distinct and characteristic excellence". It is thought that he married a daughter of the Strode family of Ravenstone. As Dean of Westminster he directed Christopher Wren's restoration of the Abbey. He moved nimbly across the political factions of his time and although he opposed the motion declaring the throne vacant in 1689 he assisted at the coronation of William and Mary. Bishop Spratt died of apoplexy on May 20th 1713 and is buried on the south side of St Nicholas' chapel Westminster Abbey. An extensive Latin inscription on the west wall of that chapel lists his achievements. Over his tomb it reads "Maxime semper valuit authoritate" (i.e. always highly valued authority). His only surviving son, Archdeacon of Rochester, was buried in the Abbey on 15th of May 1720.

The Vestry

When the school moved out of the church in 1734 the schoolroom became the Vestry room. The Vestry consisted of the Vicar, Churchwardens, Parishioners and the owners and occupiers of land in the parish. Relatively few of the members actually attended. Meetings were often held fortnightly and were concerned with many matters of local government. In 1845 the Vestry moved to the "New School Room" in East street which had previously been the workhouse. It was there that the long controversy over the pulpit took place. The Vestry took care to avoid matters costing it money. They ignored the Act of William IV requiring them to grant £150 to families wishing to emigrate. However on 25th Jan. 1849 a woman and her three children broke into the Vestry meeting and demanded her £150 which they were forced to grant. This alerted the parish and on 8.3.1849 successful claimants were: George Dawe, his wife and six children; Thomas Bugler, wife and six children and John Newbury, wife and five children. It was often difficult to get business through the Vestry. A report in the Bridport News of Saturday September 8th 1860 of the Vestry meeting of the previous Monday gives an example. Mr Swatridge, churchwarden, rose to introduce a matter concerning the fire engine but sat down shortly as all the members had hastily left bringing the meeting to an abrupt close. The Vestry behaved in much the same way as councils and committees do today. For example in 1877, with many pressing parish problems, they spent from 29th March to 9th August discussing whether a Mr Virgin should be allowed 9" of land at the fire engine house for his boundary wall. Five years later they were back discussing the fire engine house again. From 1877 the meetings were held in the National School room Hogshill street. With changes in the law the Vestry powers declined. In 1868 the power to levy compulsory church rates was abolished and in 1894 all powers passed to the new Parish Council, except the right to elect churchwardens, the control of church charities and the levy of voluntary church rates. The powers of churchwardens remained, and still exist, for example, the right of arrest. Parochial Church Councils were set up by the P.C.C.(Powers) Measure of 1921. These were modified by the Synodical Government Measure 1969, especially with respect to Team ministries.

Civil War and Commonwealth

As is well known Beaminster was burnt down, with the exception of the church and a few houses, on Palm Sunday 1644 when Prince Maurice's Irish and Flemish mercenaries rioted and set fire to the thatch in North Street whilst a strong wind swept the town. But, after the battle of Marston Moor, Fairfax, with the parliamentary army, marched to enforce the security of the south-west for Parliament. Fairfax in his diary notes; "The army marched that day (July 4th 1645) from Dorchester to Beaminster". Joshua Sprigge then took up the story in Anglia Rediva: "The train and most of the foot were quartered on the top of a hill - some few laid in Beaminster, a place of the pittifulest spectacle that man can behold - hardly a house not consumed with fire". Tradition has it that some were billeted in the church and brought their horses in with them. This is probably true since there were few other places to go. It is thought likely that this was when the mediaeval stained glass in the church was knocked out. The Army then marched on to Langport in Somerset.

The local Puritans also probably contributed. They got to the top of the tower and damaged some of the pinnacles. They were encouraged in this by the Parliamentary Ordinance of 1643 which declared that by November 1st of that year all crosses, figures etc. were to be destroyed "except monuments to King, Prince or nobleman, or other dead person who hath not commonly been reputed or taken for a saint". The figures on the North-west buttress of the church were destroyed. The springer stones remained intact apparently because they could not reach them. What is not understood is why the lower figures of the west face of the tower were unharmed. The Market Cross in the Square (properly known as the Fore place) was removed. It stood near the site of the present memorial to Julia Robinson.

The Puritan faction then set about 'ordaining' their own priests. The church of course has never recognised them and they were driven out at the Restoration. A memorandum stuck in the back of the Churchwardens Day Book of 1630 - 1674 shows what happened in Beaminster Church. Churchwardens of the time were William Mills and Samuel Hallett. The memorandum was transcribed by Richard Hine in 1906 and letters which were indecipherable were filled in from an earlier transcript by John Banger Russell.

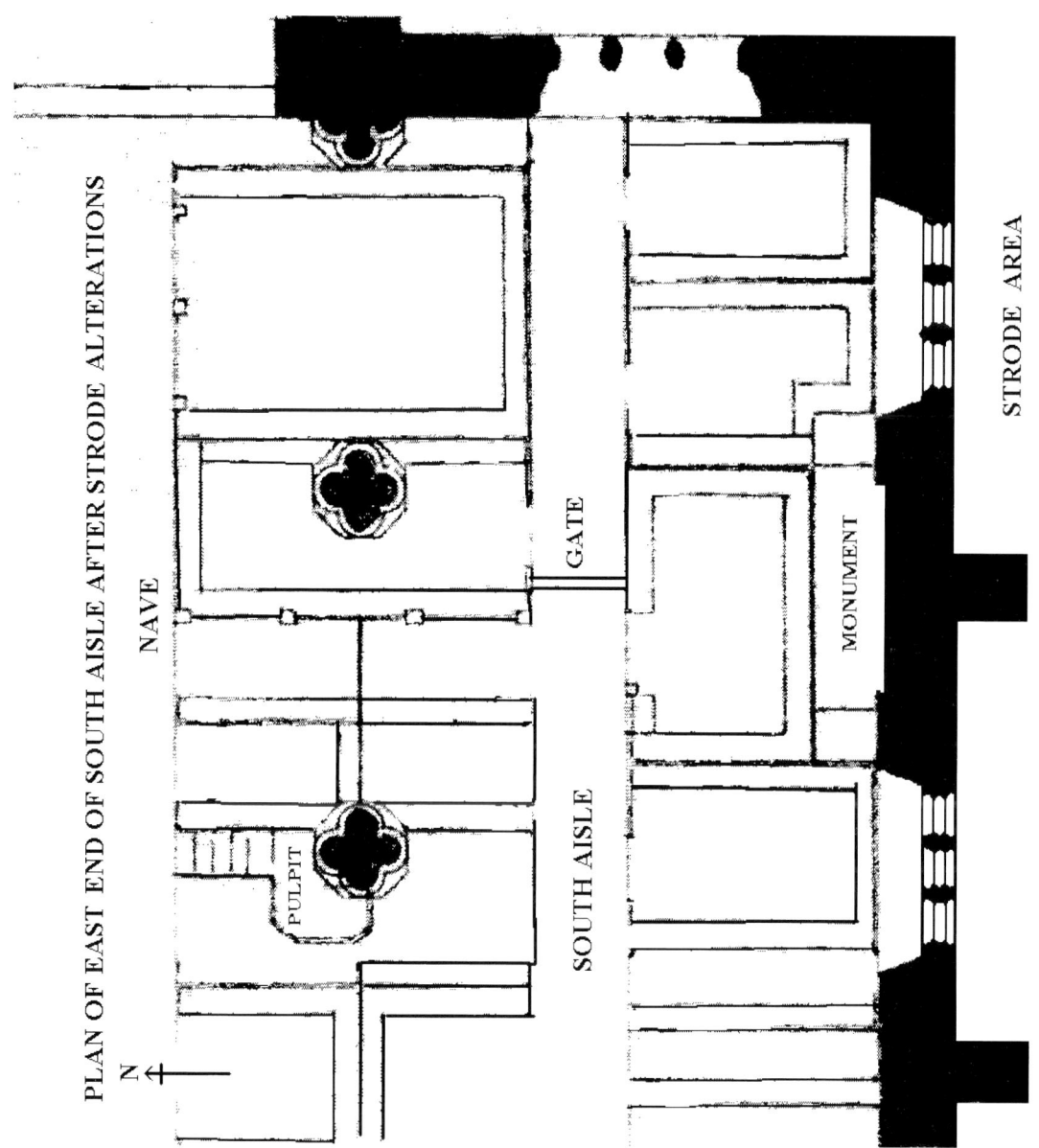

PLAN OF EAST END OF SOUTH AISLE AFTER STRODE ALTERATIONS

N

NAVE

PULPIT

SOUTH AISLE

GATE

MONUMENT

STRODE AREA

79

"EXEMPLUM.

The 14th day of May 1656 there was a solemne ordination of nine ministers in Beaminster Church where Mr Stanley Gower of Dorchester preached, Mr Short of Lime prayed, Mr Jessoppe of Wareham concluded by an exhortation after Ordinacion. The whole worke lasted from haulf an houre past eight till neere eight att after noone. 7 of the nine ministers were Curatts. They were ordeyned each by a several presbiter who proposed questions and prayed - imposition of hands was used by a competent number of the presbiters to everyone soe ordeyned, the whole worke was pformed in a solemne, godly and orderly way in a very great Assembly of Clergy and Laity.

Johes Russell".

Beaminster had very conveniently declared for Parliament during the Civil War but quickly reverted with great rejoicing at the Restoration.

The Strode Takeover

Sir John Strode of Chantmarle was buried in the church in 1642 by the bodies of his father and mother, as ordered by his will of 1637. The Churchwardens William Miles and Samuel Hallett record in the Churchwardens Book of 1646-1719 that on April 16th 1658 the eastern part of the south aisle was given to Sir John Strode in return for his giving up his seats and those of his servants elsewhere in that aisle. The Strode family proceeded to construct box pews and a vault for the burial of their dead. Sir John also bought eight seats in the gallery and other parts of the church for the use of those thus displaced. He then swept away the altar to the Virgin and St Juthware, the parclose screen that surrounded it and also the Sir John Gone blue marble altar. Only the two piscinae remain. The vault is still intact. When it was last opened in 1956 it still contained fourteen coffins. It is entered by a flight of steps from below floor level. The Strode family now placed a gate across the south aisle to restrict entry to some of their pews. It seems that this site was favoured because it was out of sight of the Vicar in the pulpit and the curtains of the pews concealed the occupants from the gaze of the 'hoi polloi'.

People today may wonder why such vandalism, for such it was, was allowed to take place. To understand that we must consider it in the context of its time. The general population were illiterate and would be unaware of what was taking place or of its implications. And in any case were powerless to intervene. The well-to-do would not interfere as they were grabbing spaces for their own box pews and some were related to the Strodes by marriage. The Vicar would not object since he owed his incumbency to the Strode family as patrons of the livings and would promptly been dismissed has he done so. Likewise the churchwardens who were tradesmen who relied for their business on patronage. The Bishop might well have stopped this had he known, but Beaminster was still in the Diocese of Bristol. Bishops rarely visited parishes in those days and there is no known record of the Bishop of Bristol visiting Beaminster. This is why virtually everyone was baptised but few ever confirmed. Finally, as we have seen, the churchwardens annual scripts, even if they had mentioned the events, were still going to the Dean of Salisbury.

In 1698 the monument to Thomas Stroud was erected at the east end of the aisle completely covering the squint and the rood loft stairs. There it remained until 1877, nearly 180 years, until it was removed to its present position which had previously been occupied by the Royal Arms. In 1746 the massive monument to George Strode and his wife Catherine was erected by the entrance to the Strode vault (see the chapter monuments and brasses).

The Monmouth Rebellion

In 1685, at the time of the Monmouth Rebellion, opinion was

divided in Beaminster. The church people in general supported James II but the non-conformists were for Monmouth. Monmouth's defeat at the battle of Sedgemoor was celebrated in Beaminster by a peal of bells and a Service of Thanksgiving was held. At least nineteen men of Beaminster had been in the rebel army and were arrested and charged with "wanting from their Homes in the tyme of the Rebellion". These included four who had been reported the previous year for non-attendance at church. They were brought before Judge Jeffreys at the "bloody assize" at Dorchester and found guilty of high treason. Four, at least, were amongst the hundreds transported to the West Indies and sold into slavery. Others were probably amongst the 320 executed. Judge Jeffreys orders were: "erect a gallows in the most public place - order faggots to burn the bowels - a cauldron to boil their heads - salt and tar them - order spears and poles for their heads when boiled in pitch". He decreed that six of the bodies were to be dispatched to Beaminster and hung from the tower as a warning to any others that might have rebellious ideas. Twelve of those found guilty were executed at Bridport and the six bodies sent to Beaminster may have come from there. The churchwardens had to find the money and see that this was carried out.

The Ghost

It seems that a ghost story is a requirement for most historic buildings and St Mary's Church Beaminster is no exception. Richard Hine in his History of Beaminster states that a ghost story had been discovered in the British museum by a Mr T. Wainwright of Barnstaple and published in the Bridport News. The original reads as follows:

"On Saturday, June 22nd, 1728, John Daniel, a lad about fourteen years of age, appeared about twelve o'clock at noon in the school at Beaminster, between three weeks and a month after his burial. The school of Beamister is kept in the gallery of the parish church, to which there is a distinct entrance from the churchyard. The key of it is every Saturday delivered to the clerk of the parish by some one or other of the schoolboys. On Saturday, June 22nd, the master had as usual dismissed his lads. Twelve of them tarried in the church-yard to play at ball. After a short space, four of them returned into school to search for old pens, and in the church they heard a noise like the sounding of a brass pan, on which they immediately ran to their playfellows and told them of it, and on their concluding that some one was concealed in order to frighten them, they all went into the school to make a discovery who it was, but on search found none. As they were returning to their sport on the stairs that led into the churchyard, they heard in the school a second noise as of a man going in great boots. Terrified at that they ran round the church, and when at the belfry or west door, they heard a third noise like a minister preaching, which was succeeded by another of the congregation singing psalms. Both the last continued but a short time. Being again at their play, in a little time one of the lads went into the school for his book, when he saw lying on one of the. benches about six feet from him, a coffin. Surprised at this he runs to his playfellows and tells them what he has seen, on which they all returned to the school-door, where five of the twelve saw the apparition of John Daniel sitting at some distance from the coffin, farther in the school. All of them saw the coffin. The conjecture why all did not see the apparition is because the door was so narrow they could not all approach it together. The first who knew it to be the apparition of the deceased was his half-brother, who, on seeing it, cried out 'There sits our John, with just such a coat on as I have' (in the lifetime of the deceased they usually were clothed alike) 'and with a pen in his hand, and a book before him, and a coffin by him. I'll throw a stone at him.' He was dissuaded from it, but did it, and doing it said 'Take it,' on which the apparition immediately disappeared, and left the church in a thick darkness for two or three minutes! On examination before Colonel Brodrepp, all the boys being between nine and twelve years of age, agreed in the relation and all the circumstances, even to the hinges of the coffin and the description of the coffin agreed to that wherein the deceased was buried. One of the lads that saw the apparition was full twelve years old, and of that age a sober sedate boy, who came to the school after deceased had left it, about a fortnight before he died, ill of the stone, and in his lifetime never had seen him. He, on examination, gave an exact description of the person of the deceased, and took notice of one thing in the apparition which escaped the others, namely a white cloth or rag which was bound round one of its hands. The woman who laid out the corpse in order to its interment deposed on oath that she took such a white cloth from the hand, it being put on it a week or four days before his death, his hand being lame. The body was found in the fields, at some distance, about a furlong beyond the house, in an obscure place, and taken up and buried without a coroner, on the mother's saying that the lad was subject to fits. But after the apparition it was dug up, and the jury that sat on it brought in their verdict 'Strangled.' They were induced to do so on the oath of two women of good repute, who deposed that two days after the corpse was found they saw it, and discovered round its gullet a black list, and likewise of the joiner, who put it into the coffin, for the shroud, not being orderly put on the corpse, but cut into two pieces, one laid under and the other over it, gave him opportunity of observing it. A chirurgeon was on the spot with the jury, but could not possibly affirm that there was any dislocation of the neck."

This could be accepted as a well authenticated story of the paranormal but there are other ways at looking at this. The established facts are few indeed: John Daniel was found dead and then buried. An inquest found that he has been strangled. No further action was taken. One detail cannot possibly be true the account of the boys crowded in the doorway and not all seeing the ghost. As the plans of the church at the time show the door opened into a lobby in front of the Mort house from there a stairway ascended to the galleries. It was not possible to see anything in the galleries until you reached the top of the stairs. At that point there was room for far more than the twenty boys. The origin of the story is obscure. Nothing seems to be known of the Mr T. Wainwright or the circumstances by which the story came to be in the British Museum. Mr Broadrepp is said to have interviewed the boys but there is no report of his findings and none was given to the inquest. The inquest took place at the King's Arms on the Square on the 6th July 1728 with a jury of twenty-four men. Thirty-eight witnesses were summoned but there is no certainty that any schoolboys were called other than two who were relatives of John Daniel or that they gave any testimony. The corpse was exhumed and the most telling evidence was that of those who had prepared the body for burial in that they had observed black marks around the throat of the dead boy. The surgeon who was called testified that the boy's neck was not fractured, which would have been evidence of a fall, but he appears rather incompetent, even with the primitive medicine of his time, in that he did not examine the larynx or thyroid cartilage for damage, which would have strongly supported strangulation. The inquest concluded that the boy had been strangled but tells nothing to authenticate the ghost story.

There is one convenient point in the story, perhaps too convenient, in that a person, who had never seen the deceased in life, described him perfectly from the apparition. However this circumstance is found in other ghost stories and seems to be a 'sine qua non' of genre. A likely scenario seems to be that friends and relatives of John Daniel, appalled that he had been buried without further action, anxious that justice be done in what they suspected to be a murder, put about stories in order to force an inquest. They probably knew more that was ever revealed publicly. The stepmother was clearly the prime suspect in that she had the motive in that she inherited the land that had been left to John Daniel; she created the opportunity by sending the boy out to Culverhayes at night; she had the means in that if she did not strangle the boy herself one of her men friends may have done it for her. The reader is left to adopt whichever explanation is preferred.

The Churchyard

The custom of interments in churchyards was introduced into England about A.D. 742 by Cuthbert, Archbishop of Canterbury, who had witnessed it at Rome. Such burials began in Beaminster with the founding of the Saxon Minster. Until 1851, when the burial-ground at Holy Trinity Church was consecrated, the graveyard around the Parish Church was the only place of interment for the inhabitants of Beaminster, save the Daniel's private mortuary at Knowle. The graveyard was used over and over again for centuries hence the need for the Mort House as a charnel house or ossuary. Matters were eased somewhat in the seventeenth century when more burials began to take place under the floor of the church. From very early days until quite recent times it was customary to bury some persons – not of the humbler rank – within the church. Sometimes the coffins were placed on shelves one above the other round a vault, but frequently a grave was dug beneath the flag-stones of the floor. Wealthy people, benefactors to the building, and often the clergy, were distinguished by interment in the chancel.

There are many entries in the Beaminster churchwardens' books of payments – "6s. 8d. for breaking the ground in the church," removal and repairs of seats, etc.

1658 "Item to John Buglar for caryinge the Rubish & earth out of the Church 0 - 0 - 6."

1713 "for taking up the stone for Mr. Hood's wife 0 -1 - 0."

The vaults greatly increased the capacity for burials as they held a number of coffins. The Strode vault, for example, holds fourteen coffins. In the eighteenth century table tombs were being constructed in the churchyard. Each consisted of a shaft going down into the bedrock with the bottom enlarged into a chamber or into a gallery. Many coffins were accommodated on shelves or rock ledges in these tombs. Each was the property of a particular family and these went on being used into the nineteenth century. A typical example is that in the south-west corner of the churchyard. It contains the coffins of Lancelot Fox, Theodore Levieux 1743, Mary his wife and daughter of John Pitts of Chard 1722, Hannah daughter of Theodore and wife of Baruch Fox 1790, Thomas Fox 1859 aged 86, Harriett his wife and daughter of Joseph Gundry of Bridport 1829, Baruch Fox, their son aged 84, Sukey his wife and daughter of John Way of Bridport 1828, Baruch Fox, son of Thomas and Harriett Fox 1863, aged 54, and several others of the family.

Until the nineteenth century little was done to improve access to the church which was by a path up a steep hill both to the north and south doors of the church. But in 1837 the entrance gates and their Ham-stone pillars were designed by Charles Coombes and erected by Waygood and Seymour. The entry in the accounts reads: "1837 July 20th Paid Messrs Waygood & Seymour for Iron Entrance Gates to the Church as per Contract £37 : 10 : 0". The Ham-stone pillars cost an additional £22. 10s. At the same time the slope was paved with stone setts and formed what is now called the 'church plane'. Shortly after steps were constructed from Church Street past the almshouse to the churchyard.

In the north-east corner of the churchyard stood the Parish Pound for the impounding of stray cattle and horses. In the churchwardens accounts for the year 1663 is the following entry: "To Gale for mendinge the pound wall 10d." also in 1666 "Paid ould Gould for menden ye church-yard wall against ye poune 1s 2d". Two old cottages together with the Round House were next to the Pound and facing the 'church plane'. The Round House was the parish lock-up where disorderly persons and drunks were confined for the night. It was built in 1831, at a cost of £40, to replace the old parish prison in East street. In 1840 these were all swept away and the churchyard enlarged. The Pound was removed to the junction of the Stoke and Broadwindsor roads. The cost of enlarging the burial ground, which included £24 to Messrs Waygood and Porter for the iron railings was £317. The cost of the consecration was £29 17s 6d. The ground was then raised to the present level.

In 1851 with the consecration of the Holy Trinity Church the new churchyard there became available. Most burials now took place there but a few internments continued in the old churchyard. In consequence of its crowded state Dr Hoffman, a Government Inspector under the Burial and Cemetery Acts, visited the churchyard in May 1818, to carry out an inspection and make a report to the Secretary of State. Following this inquiry the Inspector made this recommendation in his report; "That the churchyard be forthwith and entirely closed for Burial, except as follows: in old vaults and brick graves under certain restrictions ; in such existing earthen graves as can be opened to the depth of five feet, without exposing or displacing human remains; for the burial of widowers, widows, parents and unmarried children of those already interred therein; and in such reserved grave spaces as have never before been buried in, for so many members of the Family, as can be buried at or below the depth of five feet." In due course the graveyard was close by Order in Council.

In consequence of the increased number of cremations a faculty was obtained in 1967 to re-open the eastern part of the churchyard as a Garden of Remembrance for the internment of ashes. The first such internment took place on May 7th 1967.

The Windows

Mediaeval Windows

These were destroyed during the Cromwellian occupation. Small pieces of ancient glass remain in the cusps of the east window of the Hillary Chapel.

East and West Windows.

These are the work of William Wailes, 1808 - 81. He was a Northumbrian who began his career as a glass painter at Newcastle-on-Tyne in 1838, when he was 29. In 1841 he executed a window for Chichester Cathedral and he showed some of his work at the Great Exhibition in 1851. He was a leading pioneer in seeking to revive what was almost a lost art.

The East Window was installed in 1856 in memory of Henricus Oglander. The design of the lower third of this window is obviously inspired by Leonardo Da Vinci's mural 'The Last Supper' in the Refectory of the Convent of Sta. Maria delle Grazie in Milan. The grouping of the characters is the same but the background has been changed. The mural in Milan was well known for its 3D effect when seen from the entrance to the refectory. However the entrance has now been moved and the effect is less prominent. The Beaminster window has some three dimensional effect, particularly in early morning light if the rest of the chancel is in darkness. The rest of this window is of the usual Victorian character showing the four evangelists, scenes from the gospels etc.

Chancel - The Good Shepherd

The artist has not been traced. The inscription reads: 'To the Glory of God and in memory of Rev. Alfred Codd, Vicar of Beaminster for 33 yrs'.

East window - South aisle

John Hardman & Co of Paradise St Birmingham was employed by Pugin, who has previously employed Wailes in 1837. The output of the firm of Hardman & Co was considerable and generally of good quality. Their early windows are easily recognised by their metallic appearance which may be due to the fact that John Hardman was originally a craftsman in metal and enamel. This three light window of Jesus walking on the water is of course by Hardman and is in memory of Henry Oglander 1874.

South Aisle

The two 3 light windows are of course the work of the prolific stained glass firm Charles Kempe Studios. Charles Eamer Kempe 1837 - 1907. The three light window of St Michael, St George and St Alban is some of his early work. It is inscribed "Dominium Regem Martyrdom. Venite Adoremus". "In Honour of God and his Saints and in memory of Samuel Symes Cox. Lt.Col. 56 Regt. Mary his wife dedicates this window 1884". The three light window next - Blessed Virgin Mary, King David and St Luke is inscribed "For a remembrance before God of Thomas Russell and Mary his wife with their six children this window is dedicated A.D.1931". You have 47 years lapse between the dates of these windows. The window on the right carries the logo of C. E.Kempe and Co, the name of the firm after the death of Charles Kempe. This logo, in the lower right hand corner, consists of a sheaf and a rook (i.e. the chess piece).

The Nativity - North Aisle

Designed by Thomas Ward and Henry Hughes of Frith St Soho. From the mid 1860's until 1924 this firm remained in operation. Henry Hughes died in 1883 and the firm was taken over by a relation Thomas Figgis Curtis 1845 - 1924. It depicts the Nativity with the Blessed Virgin, Christ and Joseph. Inscribed "Gloria in Excelsis Deo". St Mary is shown, as in the other representations in the church, in the traditional blue robe. At the bottom of the window is a small pieta with the Virgin Mary, Mary Magdalene and Mary Cleophas. Its dedication reads: 'In memory of Mary Cox born on the nativity of Our Lord 1826 and dated June 3rd 1909'.

West Window

As the East window this is also the work of William Wailes. This window is entitled "Types and Prophecies". The purpose of this window is to tell the story of Advent. Starting at the top the large quatrefoil shows the Nativity with the scroll reading:

'Glory to God in the Highest and on Earth Peace, Goodwill towards Men'.

The centre six lights show the prophets that foretold the coming of Christ, Joel, Jeremiah, Isaiah, John the Baptist, Ezekiel and Daniel. They each carry a scroll with the following inscriptions:

1. In Mount Zion and in Jerusalem shall be deliverance.
2. I will raise unto David a righteous branch.
3. Behold a virgin shall conceive and bear a son.
4. Behold the Lamb of God that taketh away the sins of the world.
5. I will set up one Shepherd over them.
6. Unto Messiah the Prince shall be seven weeks.

Underneath are four theophanies, the scenes shown are:

1. The expulsion of Adam and Eve from the Garden of Eden.
2. Three angels appearing to Abraham at the door of his tent.
3. Jacob's dream.
4. Samuel anointing David.

The stone work cost £200 and was provided by Peter Cox. The tracery costing £85 and the stained glass £200 at that time was the Gift of Edward and Mary Fox of the Lodge Tunnel Road. It was installed on 11th of August 1861.

The Royal Arms and Decalogue

It was shortly after the removal of rood lofts and screens that royal arms were set up, but during the Commonwealth they were generally taken down and removed from churches. The date of the first erection of royal arms in Beaminster church is not known, the earliest entry extant refers probably to their re-erection.

Immediately following the Restoration of Charles II in 1660 it was decreed that every church should display the Royal Arms. In St Mary's they were installed on the wall of the south aisle near the altar to Sir John Gone painted on wood. The Churchwardens accounts record:

1661 Pd Henry Clarke for settinge upp of the scaffolk about ye King's armes 00 - 01 - 06.

1661 Pd William Locke in full for ye Armes 02 - 00 - 00.

A few years later it seems that the "Liorns" underwent restoration: "1677-8 gave to the men that framed the Liorns 00 - 01 - 06.

pd William Pinter for carring y" Lyon to Church 00.00. 06.

paid Hinery Peach & his men for 3 days worke for Leting in the bolsters to bare y° Liorns 00 . 06 . 00.

paid George James for Boolts & clamps for ye Liorns 00 . 16 . 00." On the accession of James II the King's Arms received further attention.

"1686 pd for an order of changing y° nams of King Charles to K. Jams" 00 - 01 - 00.

1686 Pd John Clarke for making ye frame for the King's armes and other work done about the church 02 - 12 - 04. Later they were removed to a wall under the tower.

In the refurbishment of 1862 the Royal Arms were removed altogether. Other items were also moved about the church. For example, the Decalogue:

Writing about the year 1780, J. B. Russell says – "Over the Communion Table are set up the Creed, the Lord's Prayer, & Ten Commandments in gilded letters & above is a pretty window".

For some reason, early in the nineteenth century, the Ten Commandments etc. were removed to the west end of the nave, here the tablets remained until 1846, when it appears – from the

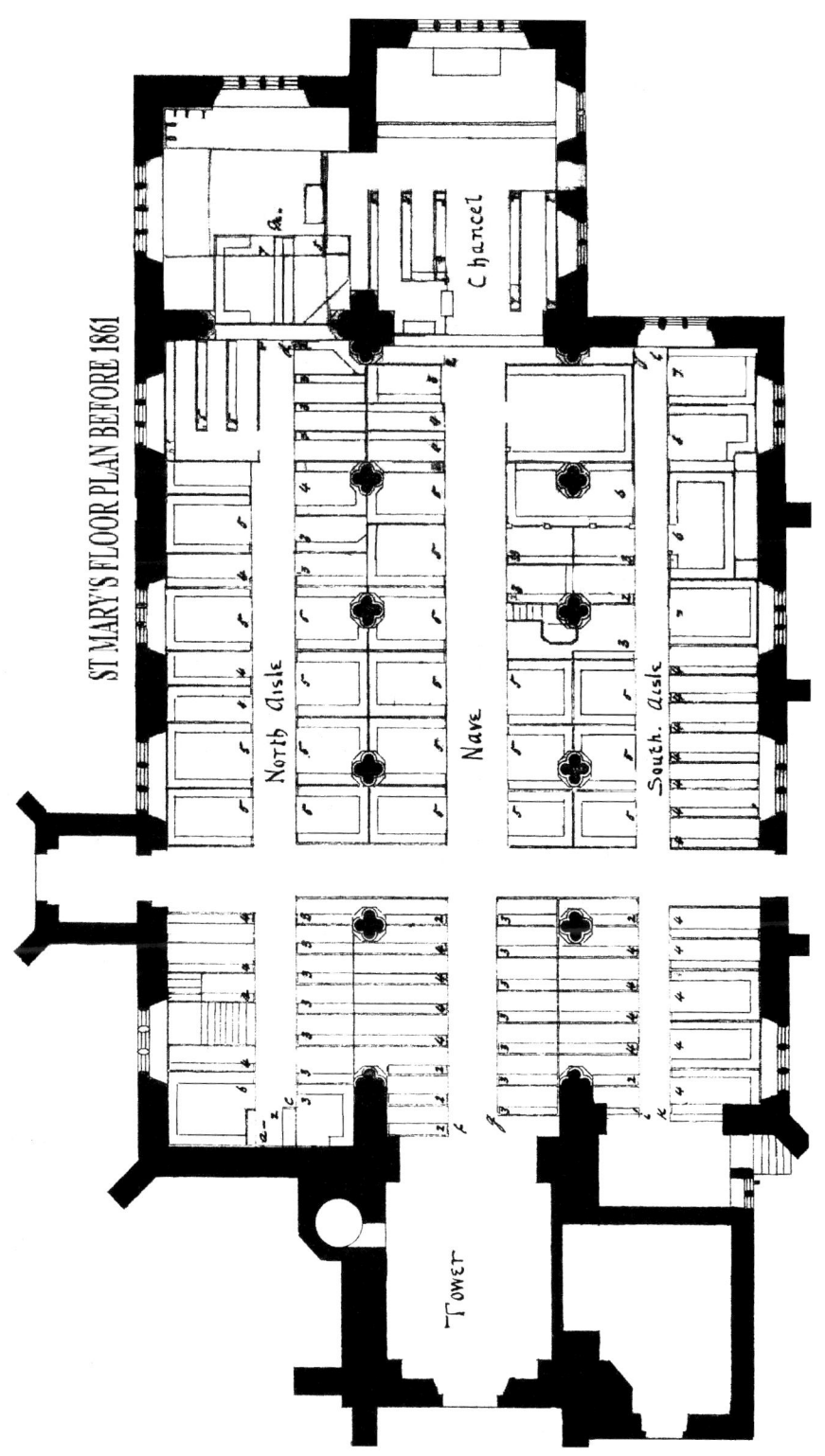

ST MARY'S FLOOR PLAN BEFORE 1861

Chancel

North Aisle

Nave

South Aisle

Tower

following entry – they were replaced in the chancel – "Jany 21st 1846. Man 3 days taking down Commandments from near West door, altring & repg. frames & fixing by side of East Window 9/-." Here the painted wooden boards remained for three years only, for in 1849 an account is rendered for "taking down Communion Railings, Wainscoting & Commandment Boards of Beaminster Chancel." Then the tablets were again fixed to the wall under the tower, where they were suffered to remain, in company with the Royal Arms, until the zeal of the "restorer" banished them all from the Church, with many other "encumbrances" in 1862.

The Corbels

In the nave of the church the eye is carried upwards by the sweep of the arches to one of the important architectural features of this church – the stone corbels supporting the roof beams. Bath stone was used as it has a finer texture and is denser than the local stone. There are four sets of corbels, three of which are quality work by Burge and his assistant Allen and were placed there in 1862-1863 during the Canon Codd restoration. Henry Burge of Winchester Street. London, who was responsible for some of the carvings in the House of Commons, was renowned for his carvings of plants and animals. The quality of the work shows in the treatment of the draperies, the careful detail and the high relief. The nave corbels depict angels carrying the implements of the passion, the symbols of kingship and the instruments of triumph. From east to west the angels carry:-

North side

1. A shield with a cross.

2. A sword.
3. A shield with three nails.

South side

12. A shield with hammer and pincers.
13. A sceptre.
14. A shield with spear and sponge.

4. A scroll.
5. A book.
6. A lute.
7. A book.
8. A harp.
9. A shield with two scourges.
10. A cross.
11. A shield and a ladder.

15. A lily.
16. A book.
17. An oboe.
18. A book.
19. A trumpet.
20. A shield with a pillar and cord.
21. A crown.
22. A shield carrying three boxes of spices for embalming.

The books no doubt represent the music of the heavenly choirs. What a focus for meditation the whole provides whilst waiting for a service to begin!

The corbels in the side aisles show Christ, the twelve apostles and the three Marys. They are as follows east to west:-

North aisle.
1. Mary Magdalene.
2. St. Peter.
3. St. John.
4. Christ.
5. St. James the Great.
6. St. James the Less.
7. St Jude.
8. The Virgin Mary.

South aisle.
1. Mary the mother of James.
2. St. Andrew.
3. St. Thomas.
4. St. Phillip.
5. St. Matthew.
6. St. Simon.
7. St. Bartholomew.
8. St. Mathias.

Burge had now run out of apostles but one corbel was left. He could hardly invent another apostle so he carved a little bird in a thicket for the last corbel. This was in a way his trademark and similar carvings can be seen in the in the Houses of Parliament. In the restoration the seventeenth century roofs of the aisles were retained and the corbels put in to support the existing beams. However an additional window was added in the north aisle. To accommodate this St James the Great had to be placed higher than all the rest and still remains so.

Perhaps the finest set of corbels are the twelve under the tower supporting the floor of the ringing chamber. They were the gift of Mr Peter Cox. In deep relief they include traditional symbols such as the Pascal Lamb, the Dove of the Holy Spirit, the Lion of St Mark and the Pelican in her Piety. There are examples of the adaptation of pagan symbols e.g. the Phoenix, which has become symbolic of the Resurrection.

Standing under the tower, looking through the south arch, the inferior corbels in the Mort House can be compared with those under the tower. Their poor quality is often excused by saying that they were the work of apprentices. This is very unlikely; they were in all probability the work of local mediaeval builders. The two which act as stops for the arch of the north door into the porch belong to the same set. The work of apprentices would not have been placed in such a prominent position.

Galleries and Pews

The internal arrangements of the church have, of course, been much influenced by the particular liturgy in use. The liturgy in turn depends to a great extent on the accepted theology of the time. In mediaeval times everyone attended Mass on Sunday but there was no seating except the few benches for the infirm as has already been said. Most of the people left the church at the Elevation of the Host leaving the priest to complete the Mass on his own. The people partook of the communion only at Easter and sometimes at Christmas. There were no books since few people could read and the Bible was in Latin which they could not understand. In fact it is problematical how much of the Christian faith they really understood because they were given little instruction. There were no sermons or music. In the Tudor period and with the coming of the Reformation things changed.

In 1544 Cranmer published the Litany in English and an order in

1547 required that the Epistle and Gospel be read in English at the Mass and that the Eucharistic vestments were to be used. The first complete Book of Common Prayer was issued in January 1549. However all this was reversed with accession of Queen Mary. On November 17th 1558, Queen Elizabeth I now being the sovereign, an Act of Uniformity was proclaimed which made the use of Edward VI second Prayer Book compulsory. Sermons now began to take a more important place in the Liturgy although they were often stilted and formal, or just read from the English Book of Homilies. A pulpit was required and in 1619 the pulpit in St Mary's was constructed.

For the fifteen years of the Commonwealth all this was abolished and the 'Directory for the Public Worship of God in the Three Kingdoms' replaced the Prayer Book. The restoration of King Charles II in 1660 brought the Prayer Book back into use and a revised edition was published in 1662 and is still in use. However sermons grew in length and began to take up to two hours to deliver. A need for seating was therefore felt. The well-to-do bought patches of the floor of the church and constructed box pews for their families. These often had canopies with curtains, couches and sometimes even a stove (the church was not heated in those days). These families vied with each other to have the grandest pew. It had long been the practice to hang family coats-of-arms and hatchments (arms of deceased persons) in the church. In the reign of Elizabeth I there were sixteen hanging there. Now these were used to hang on the canopies of the box pews. Gradually the box pews filled most of the church. Soon there were more than forty of them. For example a manuscript by Richard Symes reads:

1763 Pd the churchwardens for 10 places for myself and family behind the North door, under the gallery stairs, 10s.

1764 Expended in building my new Pews for myself and servants behind the North door in the Church of Beaminster in Workman and Materials £7 - 12 - 8d.

In June 1847 there was an advertisement in the local press announcing the sale by auction of Hitts House stating "There is a commodious Family Pew in the Church belonging to the estate".

The box pews remained until the Canon Codd 'Restoration' of 1861/3. The spread of the box pews meant that there was little room for the rest of the congregation. Those who could afford them bought bench seats and there were a few seats for the poor at the back of the church. The demand for seats led to the construction of the galleries.

In 1654 the south gallery was built. It extended only as far as the present position of the Strode monument. It had 137 seats. In 1657 the north gallery was added. This extended the whole length of the North aisle with a further 173 seats. A churchwardens book shows that seats in these galleries were sold to both men and women. In 1696 the west gallery was constructed, extending from the west wall of the church to the first pillar, and connecting the two side galleries. The pew payments were now 1s per sitting on the ground floor and 4p per seat in the galleries. There were seats for the poor under the west gallery and in all there was seating for 986 persons. Behind the west gallery was the 'ringer's larte' or belfry erected in 1765. From this belfry a door opened into the turret stair of the tower.

The north and south galleries were rebuilt in 1828 at a cost of £458 and the west gallery 'raised'. The south gallery was now known as the 'Men's gallery'. The children were seated in the west end of the south gallery next to the Mort House. Access to the galleries was by two staircases. One was close to the north door and the other from a lobby by the Mort House which opened directly into the churchyard. The west gallery was the principal one and had housed a mixed choir with six instruments - a flute, two fiddles, two hautboys and a bass viol. In the centre was a painting of David playing on a harp. In 1836 the musicians had been replaced by a small organ much to their disgust. An entry in the churchwardens accounts for

January 5th 1839 casts a little sidelight – "Pd Mr Waygood for repair of organ 2/3d". This arrangement lasted until 1861.

The Wandering Pulpit

Waves of controversy have swirled around the pulpit of St. Mary's age on age. The present pulpit is the upper tier of a three decker oak Jacobean pulpit which, in earlier times, included reading desk and clerk's desk. By its base stood the Vicarage box pew. The octagonal pulpit with enriched cornice and base moulding, fluted stem, enriched styles and two tiers of enriched arcaded panels is a good examples of the period. Originally it stood by the second pillar on the south side of the nave. Above it was a black oak sounding board. The iron hook that supported this can still be seen embedded in the stone arch. The canopy bore the inscription "To God's Glory - Richard Hillary and Lancelot Hallett built this 1619". At that time of long sermons an hour glass was provided to time the preacher. In the churchwardens accounts for 1650 we read "Disbursements : paid for a Hower Glasse 00-01-00".

It was the custom of the time for people to play various games in the churchyard, much to the annoyance of the puritans. Following the suppression of these games by the Lancashire magistrates in 1617 James I and later Charles I in 1633 ordered a declaration to be read from the pulpit on Sunday after divine service in favour of certain lawful sports. This was known as the Book of Sports. Bettey tells us in "Church and Community" that Mr Spratt, curate, having, unwillingly, read the declaration after evening prayer from the pulpit, preached against the royal declaration. This upset local people but apparently made little difference as Beaminster people continued to play their favourite game of fives in the churchyard. In 1839 gas lighting was introduced into the church and a special sermon was preached on the occasion by the curate of Corscombe. His remarks about dissenters aroused much controversy. A pamphlet was published entitled "The Question Answered; 'Can Dissenting Congregations Claim the Blessings promised to United Worship' including remarks on a sermon recently delivered in Beaminster Church by Rev W Maskell A.M. Curate of Corscombe - By Alfred Bishop Beaminster. In magnis veritas, in aliis libertas, in omnibus charitas. Printed by J. Price Bridport 1839. The translation is 'In great matters truth, in others freedom, in everything charity'. Mr Bishop was pastor of the Congregational Chapel. However more contentious matters were yet to come. In 1844 the pulpit was removed to the front of the chancel and in 1848 the sounding board and canopy disappeared. The accounts of the period state "Taking down the head of the pulpit 2/6". So began a controversy that was to last for nearly twenty years. In 1851 the Rev. Samuel Flood and the churchwardens had the pulpit taken down, mutilated and re-erected in the chancel. Records state that this was "much to the vexation of the townspeople". At the Easter vestry on April 13th 1852 the accounts were passed only upon the churchwardens apologising and admitting publicly that they had exceeded their authority by removing the pulpit without the consent of the parish. Mr J.P. Dowdeswell and Sir James W. Schroedde were the churchwardens. However the pulpit remained in the chancel. A vestry meeting on 3.3.1853 with the Rev. Alfred Richings, now vicar, in the chair rejected unanimously the siting of the pulpit in the chancel. Thomas Russell and John Furmedge proposed that the pulpit be restored to its former position in the same character and form in every respect. This was carried but in the meantime the passage of the accounts was withheld. A public meeting a week later decided that "the churchwardens were to return the pulpit and report, subject to the Ordinary at the next confirmation to be held here, and on obtaining license and consent, carry out the same and agree with persons whose sittings and pews had been disturbed by such removal". The next week the Vestry decided that a memorandum be presented to the

Bishop with reference to the removal of the pulpit. Finally the accounts were passed. A few days later the churchwardens were replaced by Peter Cox and Daniel Ackerman. On May 10th the Bishop replied that the pulpit might as well stay where it was. The Bishop now died.

A meeting on 21st April 1854 proposed that the memorandum now be presented to his successor without delay. In August of that year a further motion to return the pulpit was agreed with the additional proviso that it be not moved without reading desk and clerk's desk. The Bishop, however, upheld his predecessor's decision. If anyone now thought that this was the end of the matter they had reckoned without the people of Beaminster.

On 13th April 1855 the churchwardens were requested to write to the Bishop to ask if it was his final decision that the pulpit remain despite the resolution of a large majority of the parish and of the present meeting on the grounds that they could not hear the sermons. The churchwardens were also to enquire into the proper procedure for taking the business of the pulpit through the Bishop's Court. The matter dragged on for some time. However in 1856 the patched up pulpit minus the clerk's desk was restored to its former site in the nave. In the restoration of 1862 the reading desk was swept away and the pulpit set on a new base and moved to the north pier of the chancel arch. There it remained until by a faculty granted on 14th October 1970 the north aisle altar was installed and the pulpit moved to the first pillar on the south side and new steps provided for it. A further faculty on 21.12.81 provided for a westward extension of the chancel step and the moving of the pulpit to the south aisle. Finally in 1986, with funds provided by the Mothers Union, the pulpit was placed on castors thus enabling it to be moved to suit a changing liturgy. It was from this pulpit that the Services of Humiliation were preached in the 18th century. These were in response to severe epidemics that swept the district killing man and beast. The disease was anthrax which, because of the very resistant spores of the bacillus, recurred

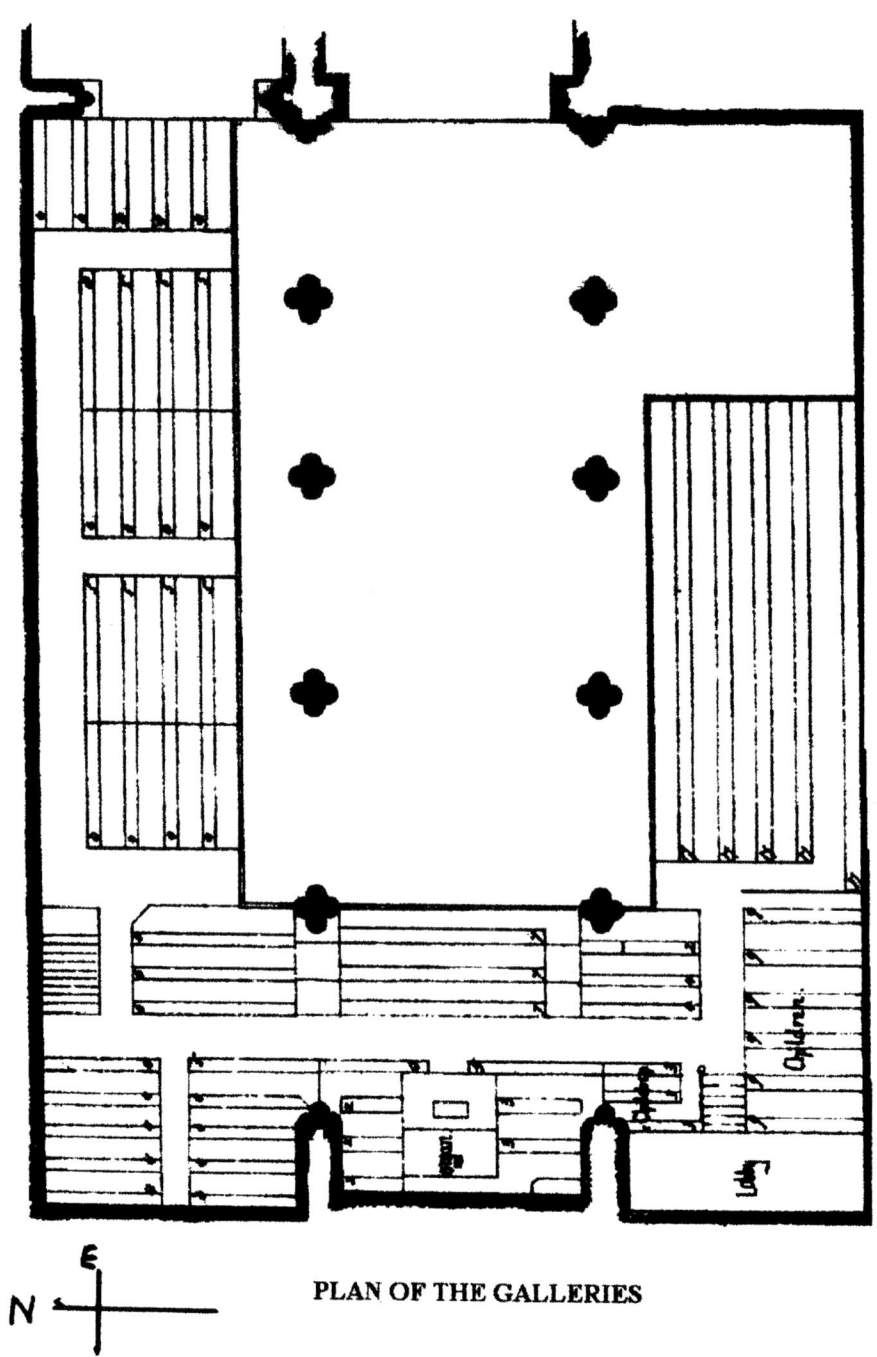

PLAN OF THE GALLERIES

a number of times. At the time the cause was unknown and not discovered until 1863. Beaminster was particularly prone to the disease because the wool used in serge making and hides in tanning carried it. Services of Humiliation are not to be confused with Services of Commination provided for in the 1662 Prayer Book. The latter consisted of a denunciation of God's anger against sinners. The former were to encourage the population to humble itself in the face of the disease visitation. The Services of Humiliation were preceded by a distribution of handbills calling the people to church. These ended with a statement that those who did not attend, without good reason, must be considered accursed.

Canon Codd's Restoration

What is commonly called Canon Codd's Restoration of the church was not in fact a restoration at all. It was an extensive repair and reorganisation. Canon Alfred Codd M.A. succeeded Cornelius Ritchings B.A. as Vicar on July 15th 1857, who had become Vicar following the resignation of Samuel Flood on October 9th 1852. He found the church considerably neglected. Maintenance and repairs had not been carried out except for the building of the north porch in 1830. All attention had gone to the new Holy Trinity Church. The interior was still full of box pews when it was no longer considered right that people should 'own' part of the floor. Moreover the galleries were no longer necessary. Part of the population were worshipping at Holy Trinity and the population was gradually declining in number. The worsted trade had disappeared more than ten years earlier and little was now left of sailcloth manufacture since the navies of the world had gone over to steam. There was no vicarage so Canon Codd moved into Barton End in Fleet Street.

Canon Codd had no difficulty in obtaining faculties for the numerous works that were required but he met with considerable

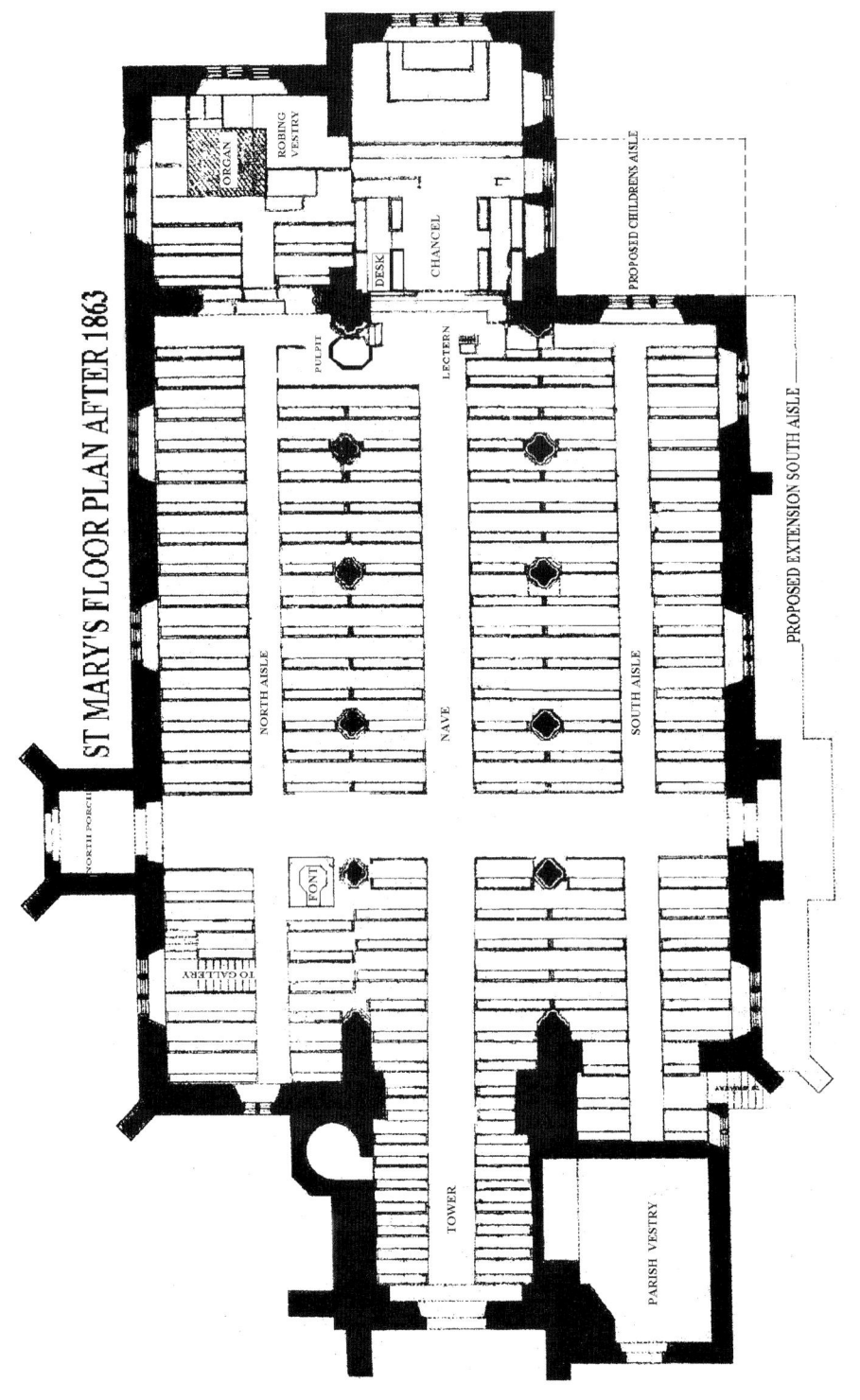

ST MARY'S FLOOR PLAN AFTER 1863

NORTH PORCH

TO GALLERY

NORTH AISLE

FONT

PULPIT

ORGAN

ROBING VESTRY

DESK

CHANCEL

LECTERN

NAVE

SOUTH AISLE

TOWER

PARISH VESTRY

PROPOSED CHILDREN'S AISLE

PROPOSED EXTENSION SOUTH AISLE

Architect plans south elevation

opposition. This was not because the parishioners objected to the work but because the money had to be raised by levying a church rate which had to be passed by the Vestry. The rate was charged on property and the Vestry consisted almost wholly of property owners . The first most urgent work needed was repair of all the roofs. The Vestry met in early December 1861 but made no decisions. The meeting met again on 27th December and again there were no agreements. In view of this a Parish Meeting was called on January 25th 1862 but the proposition to proceed with repairs was defeated by 81 votes to 24. However on the 1st of February the Vestry agreed to receive an estimate from Hicks of Dorchester for £550 to cover the roofs of nave and aisles with 7mil sheet lead. This was agreed unanimously as was a decision to levy a five farthing Church Rate. but a further meeting on 6th March refused to go ahead with this and declined to advertise for further tenders by 18 votes to 16. Mr Peter Cox now proposed that he should raise a loan of £600 at 5% interest, the Principal and Interest to be paid by ten yearly instalments. This was accepted and the various works went ahead. The roofs were repaired and the skylights over the chancel removed. A ventilator was installed in the middle of the nave roof. The roof timber forming the ceiling of the nave was replaced but the roof timbering of the aisles was left intact in its original form. The corbels supporting the roof beams were renewed. Masons prepared blocks of Bath stone at a cost of £9 18s 0d and Henry Burge, of Winchester Street London was commissioned to cave them. The galleries were now removed and all the box pews. They were all replaced by bench pews. However the soft wood from the galleries and from some old cupboards was used in the construction and this stored up trouble for the future. Whilst this was being done the flagstone floor was removed and replaced with wood. All this virtually put the church out of action and most services including weddings and baptisms had to be transferred to Holy Trinity. The first child to be baptised there was Alfred Codd's first-born son Alfred Percy Codd on 17th December 1857. However when the Bishop got to hear of this he sent a letter of complaint pointing out that Holy Trinity was not licensed for this purpose. In due course a license was granted.

Attention was now turned to the Mort House. The upper storey was removed by W & R Chambers and also the doorway from the churchyard by the last buttress of the church. The walls were now levelled and a new roof provided. An archway was now installed giving entrance to the ground floor. That this arch is later than others in the church can be seen in that it is not a panelled arch. The Great West Window and the west window of the North Aisle needed attention. New tracery and the stained glass for the Great West Window was provided by donors. The stone tracery which had been of the Perpendicular form with narrow lozenge openings in the tracery was replaced with a more open tracery matching the windows of the rest of the church. The window in the North Aisle was unblocked (it had been boarded up for many years) and its tracery left in original Perpendicular form. An additional window was provided to the immediate east of the north door and the niche that originally held a stoup was preserved. The old organ, having been removed from the west gallery, was discarded. A new organ was purchased for £325 but this too was replaced in 1863. Little change was made to the chancel but the altar rails were renewed and the wrought iron panels below the rails are the work of Mr Tardene of Bideford and installed on 4th June 1861. The pulpit was set up on a new base by the north pillar of the chancel arch. In May 1861 a new ringer's floor and a new chimes floor were constructed in the tower. The ringing floor cost £31 10s 0d and the chimes floor £60 16s 0d. The ringers being moved to the first floor made room for more pews under the tower. These were for children and, being free, for the less well off adults. The church could now seat 600 people. Despite generous donations from individuals the cost was £3,000 and the Church Rate went up to

4d in the pound. At a meeting on June 23rd 1864 a Vestry for fixing the Church Rate, with eighteen members present, negatived any proposal for raising the rate. However in due course, after much haggling the rate was fixed.

In Victorian times many people believe that theirs was the most advanced society that had ever existed. Therefore it was logical, it seemed to them, to pull down old buildings, and that included churches, and rebuild them in Victorian Gothic. The Church Architect at this time, Mr William White of Wimpole Street London, was certainly one of these. One of his first acts was to throw out the Norman font. It was replaced with a Victorian font which was purchased by funds raised in a campaign by Miss Jane Keddle, a Sunday School teacher for many years and eldest daughter of Dr Keddle physician. He built the new vicarage in that style but was foiled in his ambition to do the same with the church. He made his intentions quite clear in the drawings he made for projected 'improvements'. The drawing reproduced here, dated January 1861, shows his proposal to pull down the south aisle and rebuild it with the wall further out and to extend it alongside the chancel. This extension was to hold the children. Then he proposed removing the nave roof, carrying the walls higher and inserting six clerestory windows on each side. All this was prevented because of lack of funds. With the departure of much industry the town was much poorer than it had been so Mr White's schemes were never approved.

The building work did not finish there as various smaller jobs were carried out plus all the work that has been described on the tower. Until 1887 the turret stairs were entered from a door on the ground floor under the tower. It was then blocked up and the outside steps and entrance made. Hearsay has it that the ringers had this done because they could then slip away after ringing, without attending the service, which they could hardly do when they came down into the church.

Church Baumgarten : Scale 8 feet to an Inch : No 8

South Elevation :

Proposed New Chancel Aisle for Children
& side Galleries are removed.

108

The Organ and Choir

When the galleries were removed in 1861 they had been in place for 200 years having been erected in the years 1654 - 1657. With the removal of the west gallery went the organ. A faculty was obtained in 1861 to remove the organ from its gallery under the western arch and replace it with one in the Hillary chapel. The organ having been removed with the western gallery, a new organ of two manuals was installed in the centre of the Hillary chapel in 1863. It was built by Halmshaw and Sons of Birmingham and cost £1,269. The old organ was removed to the girls schoolroom - then in east street and in 1866 this organ was sold and some years later was re-erected in the Wesleyan chapel. In 1911 the organ was again removed and replaced with new parts and parts of the old organ including the case and pipes. It was placed in the western half of the Hillary chapel. This organ, which cost only £50 more than the earlier one, was supplied by Messrs Hele of Plymouth.

At the opening service on Oct 18th the Bishop of Worcester performed the dedication and the organist Mr T.R. Pine played for the service. Afterwards a recital was given by Mr W.W. Trotman. B.A. of Torquay. The collection was for the damaged pinnacles. This organ was blown by a hydraulic mechanism. While excavating for the water pipes a brass shield from a coffin was found which read "William Clarke Esq. Died April 17th 1811. Aged 12 years" together with fragments of others.

In 1955 a proposal was made to rotate the organ through 90 degrees and move the choir out into the north aisle. This was put off for a year on grounds of lack of finance but there were also a number of objections. In 1957 the proposal was made again on the grounds that it would make more vestry room. Again no action was taken. In June 1959 the organ was overhauled. At the Annual Meeting in 1961 the Vicar, the Rev. J.S. Arthur, announced that there would be an experiment with the choir. At Lent it would be moved out into the church. This was carried out but lasted only six months because it was found to be so unsatisfactory. The choir returned to the chancel but two years later it was tried again. This time the experiment lasted less than three months. In 1966 it was proposed to move the organ under the tower. A remote consol was suggested to keep the choir at the east end because of the objections. This was abandoned on 2nd of March 1967. In April 1968 the organ was taken apart, cleaned and rebuilt. This was complete by September 1968.

In July 1998 a petition was made for a faculty to move the choir and build new choir stalls in the north aisle and provide a remote consol. On the posting of the Citation there were 520 objectors from the parish. Some thought that this should not be so as many were not church people. But as the Care of Churches Ecclesiastical Jurisdiction Measure makes clear, anyone resident in the parish of whatever denomination, or none, and anyone on the electoral roll although not resident in the parish can vote on a matter concerning the church building itself and its ordering. The objectors were prepared to take the matter to the Consistory Court. Legal opinion was that the objection would almost certainly have been upheld. The petition was withdrawn. Later it was proposed that the choir stay in the chancel but a consol be provided near the central altar. Nothing has been done to implement this proposal so far.

Monuments and Plaques

The oldest monument in the church is that erected by the Strode family in memory of Thomas Strode in 1698. It is by Peter Scheemakers, an eminent monumental sculptor of the eighteenth century, of marble in the baroque style. His work is considered to be of good technical quality. It is wall mounted but the pilasters and supporting cornice projecting from the tabulation provide the space

Thomas Strode

for a larger than life size sculpture of Thomas Strode as a standing figure in wig and gown. The whole is fronted with the traditional putti which are often mistaken for cherubs and surmounted by Thomas Strode's coat of arms. The Latin inscription starts and finished with an acronym. Today acronyms are more usually found as names for computer components or languages. The first D.O.M.P.Q expands to Domine Optimo Maximo Potentissimo Que whilst the second L.M.D.P.Q. gives Liberi Monumentum Dederunt Posuerunt Que but this has also been rendered as Libens Merito Dicavit Posuit Que. The whole Latin text now becomes:

Domine optimo maximo potentissimoque . Mortalitatis exuvias hic deposite THOMAS STRODE, Serviens et legem: Qui in Christo placide obdormovit Feb. 4th 1698. Aetat fuae 70. Vir Immortali Memoriae Sacratus; Jurisprudentia, pietate, et consilio, Insignis. Moribus Integris Juxta et Suavissimis; Deo, Principi, et amicus semper fidus; Patre Johane Strode Equite, Aurato de Parnham in Comitatu Dorset oriundus Charissimam fili adscivit Conjugem, Mariam Adams, relic de Parkinson Odber, Amerigo. Ex qua filiam suscepit unicam adhuc superstitem. Quae hoc supremu pietatis Monument Maestissima et cum lacrymis gemens.Libens merito dicavit posuitque.

This translates:

"To the Glory of the Most High Almighty God. Here lie the mortal remains of Thomas Strode, Serjeant-at-Law, who fell peacefully asleep in Christ on Feb. 4th 1698, in his 70th year. A man sacred to immortal memory; distinguished in jurisprudence, sense of duty and judgement; of character upright as it was eminently agreeable; always faithful first to God, and to his friends; a worthy son of his father John Strode Knight of Parnham in the county of Dorset. He took as his beloved wife Mary Adams, widow of Parkinson Odber, Esquire, by whom he had an only daughter, still surviving, who in deep grief and with tears and sighs and filial affection, willingly set up and dedicated this memorial of a good life". Various translations of memorial inscriptions in the church have been published and often they have been more florid than the inscriptions themselves.

After the death of George Strode in 1753 the large free standing monument in black and white marble was erected to him and his wife Catherine. It is also the work of Peter Scheemakers and stands just above the Strode vault. This is an example of his classical style. In his book 'Highways and Byways in Dorset', published in 1906, Sir Frederick Treves, the royal surgeon, thought that the ladies shown were the wife Catherine at the death bed of her husband and two daughters dressed up in classical style. As was so often the case he was quite wrong, which is not surprising since he described Broadwindsor as being in the centre of a singularly featureless plain! He severely criticises the work no knowing that the sculptor was acclaimed at the time. One can only suppose that he was more competent when he removed King Edward VII's appendix. The ladies represent Faith, Hope and Charity, carrying the traditional symbols. In any case Catherine could hardly have attended the deathbed of her husband as she died seven years before him as the inscription in English makes quite clear. The only other monument in the south aisle is a marble plaque in memory of one Stephen Atkinson dated Nov. 6th 1839 of whom nothing seems to be known.

The north aisle contains several monuments which cast light on the history of Beaminster. At the west end is the War Memorial. This consists of a slab of Portland stone weighing over a third of a ton carved with the names of the thirty-four Beaminster men who fell in the First World War and the names of the fifteen killed in the Second World War . The monument was designed by Gordon Hake ARIBA. It was installed on December 26th 1920 with considerable ceremony. The cost of the memorial was £175. 11s. 0d.

Nearby is the Samways memorial. This is of Purbeck stone and black slate with Corinthian pilasters. It is not in its original position having been moved from the north side of the chancel about 1863.

The inscription in gold letters on the slate reads:

[Mors Janua Vitae]

In Memoriam Henrici Samwayes Gen. qui Obiit 22° die Julii. Aetatis Suae 60° Dominiq. Anno : 1706.° Et quinq. filiorum, Iohannis, Thomae, Georgii, Garlandi, et Roberti, in pueritia morte correptorum. Ac etiam Henrici filii natu maximi, qui e vita excessit 25° die Augusti, Anno 1711° et .Aetat: suae 35° Et Mariae filiae Unicae Liberorum Ultimae, et Aegidii Merefeild Gen : Uxoris quae animam efflavit Iulii 18° die A.D. 1712° et Aetat : suae 23° Quinq. vident nuptam Lunae, tumuloq. sepultam. Johanna Samwayes, vidua, hoc Monumentum conjugalis et materni amoris indicium perenne erexit, post funera infra depositas esse reliquias nequaquam in futuro removendas exoptans. In translation:

Death is the Gate of Life.

In memory of Henry Samwayes, Gentleman, who died the 22nd day of July aged 60 years in the year of Our Lord 1706. And of his five sons John, Thomas, George, Garland and Robert snatched away by death in childhood. And also Henry the first born son, who departed this life the 25th day of August in the year 1711 in his 35th year. And Mary, his only daughter and the last of his children, wife of Giles Merefeild, Gentleman, who breathed out her life the 18th day of July 1712 in her 23rd year. Five months saw her married and buried in the tomb. Joan Samwayes, the widow, erected this monument as a lasting token of her wifely and motherly love earnestly desiring that the mortal remains, which after the funeral were deposited below this place shall in future never be removed.

The members of this family all died within the space of six years. This high mortality was general in Beaminster families at the time. This was due to Anthrax an epidemic which swept the town several times in the eighteenth century. It was brought in on the wool and skins of the sheep whose wool was used in the worsted trade and skins brought to the Tanyard close to the church. Pasteur's work was still in the future so nothing was known of the germ theory of disease. A number of useless regulations were made by the authorities which failed to effect any control. The disease finally disappeared after the woollen industry moved to Yorkshire with the invention of power driven looms. Beaminster suffered further epidemics due to meningitis in 1919, polio in 1923 and diptheria in 1938. Dr Pim, Medical Officer of Health, early in the 20th century said "that with open drains and lack of a sewage system it was a wonder that we were not swept by bouts of typhoid." Perhaps we all survived thanks to a high natural immunity.

Opposite is an undated memorial of white marble with black marble pilasters and armorial bearings above. This is in memory of John Hoskins and his only daughter Mary Gifford.

John Hoskins had a considerable estate and his daughter married into the Gifford family in 1685, leases of the Langdon estate and involved with the industry in the town. Moving eastwards the next monument in marble dated 1793 is that of Richard Symes barrister and his family . An oval medallion depicts a carved female figure leaning on a draped urn with armorial bearings below inscribed:

"In Memory of Richard Symes, of Beaminster Esqr. Barrister at Law, who departed this life the eighth day of Novr. 1783, Aged 57 years. Also of Elizabeth his Wife, who departed this life the 10th day of May 1792. Aged 62 years. And of Ann, their only issue, and of Samuel Cox, Esqr. her Husband He departed this life on the 20th day of April 1822, Aged 63 years. She on the fourth day of Sept. in the same year, Aged 52 years". In the 1970s a thief removed the armorial plaque with a chisel. Some months later the police apprehended this thief in Bristol. He had in his possession a collection of these coats of arms all neatly labelled with the names of the churches from which they had been stolen. This item was then returned to Beaminster and the monument restored.

John Banger Russell Memorial next is of white marble framed with black marble. J.B. Russell is particularly remembered for his manuscripts recording history of the town. Inscription: Memoriae sacrum Johannis Banger Russell. vir inter suos examinae morum comitatis. Inter alios probitatis summae. In doctnna forensi, et universa literaria Celeberrimi. Qui vitam ea sapientia instituerat. Ut extrema sustenaret ea fiducia. Quam nil nisi vera pieta impertire posset. Obiit die Mai XXV A.D. MDCCCXXVII annos sexaginta et septem natus.

Which reads: Sacred to the memory of John Banger Russell; a man of extraordinary pleasantness of manner amongst his friends, and amongst everybody else. A man of the highest integrity. Distinguished in forensic practice and all literature, who conducted his life with such wisdom that he sustained his end in the trust of it, which nothing except true piety could impart.

Strangely there is no memorial to Thomas Russell of another Russell family in Beaminster who was also a solicitor and a poet. A Fellow of New College Oxford it is recorded that he was "at an early age master of the dead languages and almost all the living ones".

The Purbeck stone wall monument is in memory of Gershom son of Theodore Levieux. Theodore was the son of a rich family of goldsmiths with a business in Montpelier but he became a Huguenot and with the Revocation of the Edict of Nantes by Louis XIV in 1685 had to flee the country. It is often asked why he came to Beaminster? The answer is because Beaminster was known far and wide as the maker of linen sailcloth and also serge. As the Sun Life Insurance records show he set up as a serge maker in the town and a policy for his workshops is dated 1738. On 2.2.1693 he married Mary daughter of the vicar Peter Bnce. In addition to the son Gershom born in 1694 there were two daughters Maria and Hannah. In 1722 his wife died and later Theodore married again. The second marriage was very unhappy and upset his daughters who soon married and left home. In his will Theodore decrees that the second wife shall have not a single item of his property or possessions and shall be out of the house within one year of his death. Maria married John Slade of

Colliton on 19.11.1741 and Hannah married Baruch Fox of the Southgate family of lawyers on 6.8.1744. This entry is in error in the Netherbury registers. Baruch is spelt wrongly and is shown as from Sherborn(sic). The history of the Fox family is well known and the error is evident. Sherborne may have been a misreading of a badly written Southgate. Theodore, his first wife, Hannah and Baruch Fox are all buried in the family table tomb in the south-west corner of the churchyard. Three Fox family members called Baruch appeared in successive generations. Theodore's will and insurance policy are important since they tell in detail the contents of his house and workshop at the time.

The remaining monument in this aisle of white and grey marble with shield of arms and standing female figure leaning on an urn is to three brothers of the Cox family. It reads: **In memory of** Daniel Cox Merchant, who died 23rd Oct. 1778, Aged 57 Years, Also of John Cox Surgeon, who died 28th November 1783, Aged 55 Years. And of Samuel Cox, Merchant, their elder Brother, who in his Life time, caused this Monument to be erected. He died 28th April 1801. Aged 82 Years. This was a prominent family in the eighteenth century. They owned several of the local farms. Samuel was Lord of the Manor and donated the land on which the Holy Trinity Church was built. This monument was removed from the chancel and placed in its present position in 1862.

No doubt in time past, many ancient memorial brasses have been removed from the church, some perhaps sold as old metal, others stolen. In the churchwardens' accounts for the year 1669, is the following entry – "To the scot for taking of the Brass from Mr. Hardyes Tomb 6d." The brasses were removed and sold in 1861/2 and were "lost" for 50 years. However they appeared in a public auction in the town in 1913 and the purchaser returned them to the vicar (Canon Hutchings). Unfortunately the only ones replaced in their correct positions were the four in the Hillary chapel that in the chancel in

The Chancel before 1912

memory of Emily Codd, widow of Rev. Canon Codd. 1908. "That they all may be one" and those below the windows. Apart from three recent plaques all the others are misplaced. In the south aisle there is one inscribed "Here lies the body of Joseph Symes departed this life Mar. 27th 1776 aged 75 years and Frances his wife Sep. 9th 1737 aged 47 years" and another "Here lies the body of Elizabeth Smitham who departed this life Dec. 30th 1773, aged 61 years". In the north aisle one reads "Underneath lieth the body of William Brinson who departed this life 11th day of August 1723 in the 50th year of his age" and another "Here lyeth the body of Margerie Mason, the wife of John Mason, who died the 2nd Feb. 1591".

Apart from those attached to the stained glass windows there are four recent plaques. One in memory of Canon George Cyril Hutchings M.A. (1912 - 1943) on the front of the choir stalls, This one is almost obliterated by continual enthusiastic polishing. The whole of the choir stalls was, in fact, dedicated to his memory. In the north aisle one brass plate is inscribed: "In loving memory of Cecil Collins Hann, killed in action in the air Oct. 22nd 1916, aged 25 years. Body laid to rest at Heilly, Mericourt L'Abbe, France. Greater love hath no man than this, that a man lays down his life for his friends. St John XV.13. The other plate reads: "In memory of Herbert Arnold Lake, 1883 - 1969, Physician for 49 years. Churchwarden for 19 yrs 1946 - 1965. The remaining brass plate is attached to the altar rails of the north altar and reads: "In memory of Haigh Clive Rybot 1874 - 1929 and his wife Linda Mabel 1866 - 1956". Another dedication in the church is the modern lectern made at Beaminster School in memory of Mrs Skyrm (1879 - 1969). Mrs Skyrm was the wife of Llewellyn Skyrm M.A. headmaster of Beaminster & Netherbury Grammar School.

The Screens

Another feature of St. Mary's Church is the chancel screen; it was installed in 1912 and dedicated in 1913 in memory of the Rev. Arthur Leonard. A heavy stone screen had been designed for the restoration of 1862/3 but fortunately this was never built. The present screen of English oak was designed by Charles Ponting of Marlborough and carved by H. Read Of Exeter. The Rood Cross was installed at the same time but under a separate faculty and this is a reminder of the rood loft of mediaeval times. The churchwardens at the time were Messrs J.L. Kitson and A.V. Pine. At the time of its installation critics said " There was no feature which would so greatly enrich the church".

To appreciate its artistic merit it is necessary to inspect it in detail. The screen was designed for its position in this particular church.

It is, of course, generally in the perpendicular style. However there are various elaborations. The tracery under its arches, for example, whilst maintaining the general theme, contains eight small birds, most beautifully carved, engaged in various activities such as feeding their young. The running vine frieze reflects the vine motif of the 15th century pillars of the nave. This is made of nine separate panels and although, at first sight, the design seems to be repetitive closer examination reveals that each panel is unique in conception and yet maintains the overall balanced effect. Here we have quality in both conception and execution - even the acanthus bosses out of sight in the rear are finely wrought.

The four evangelists who are shown on the front of the screen are depicted with the usual symbolism. St Matthew the tax-gatherer carries his money bag and St John the poisoned chalice of legend. The story behind this is that St John was once presented with a poisoned chalice of wine. When he blessed the chalice the poison left the wine or became harmless. St Mark as the author of the earliest

The Chancel circa 1934

gospel is shown with a book. This, however, is an anachronism, books of this kind did evolve during the first centuries of the Christian Era. Indeed in the 4th century letters of St Jerome there is reference to a book with jewelled covers. However books of the type shown did not exist at the time of St. Mark, there being either scrolls or loose collections of sheets. St Luke, the physician, however, is carrying a scroll. Does this represent his gospel or was it a prescription? The rood cross is flanked by two crocketted pinnacles which echo those on the tower.

It is often said that the screen is responsible for poor acoustics in the chancel and blocking the sound of the choir from the nave. In fact complaints were being made about the acoustics long before the screen was installed. At the height of the choir the chancel arch is 153 inches wide.

The screen supports occupy just 18 of those inches. Some measurements were made in the early 1980's and it was found that the sound attenuation was not due to the screen but to the general acoustics of the church.

The screens in the western arch and the mort house arches replace those removed in 1870. They are of English oak and match the wardrobes in the under tower space installed at the same time 1994. The screen in the western arch conceals a rolled steel joist which was included to add stability to the structure.

Church Silver

Over the centuries the church has received many gifts of silverware. However none now exists earlier than the eighteenth century. The present silver is as follows:
A pair of Flagons 56oz each made by Thos Whipham
    London in 1739, gift of George Strode in 1749.
A pair of Patens 9oz each by William Peaston 1749 gift of

The 1854 Chalice

George Strode.

A Chalice 13oz by Fuller White London 1749.

A Chalice 7oz London maker (Phillip Rollos?) 1797

A Chalice 8oz & Decanter (glass & silver filigree) by George Angel London 1845.

A Paten depicting Apostles 22oz by J & G Angel gift of Mrs E. Fox. 1846

A Chalice with Apostles 24.5oz by Joseph Angel gift of Mary Cox 17.6.1854

Two Anointing spoons silver & plate 1850.

A Salver 31oz by J & W Barnard London. Gift of Sam & Mary Cox 1884

A Priest's Paten 8oz Silver plate 1899 the gift of the Parish of Chilvers Cotton.

A Wafer Box 7.5oz by J & W Ltd London 1905.

A Wafer Box 10oz (Birmingham) in memory of K.J.P. 1927.

A Chalice & Paten 24oz by F.G. London 1963 in memory of Peter Bailey.

A Ciborium 19oz 1973 (London) in memory of Harold Gibson.

A Ciborium 8oz 1987 by C & S Sheffield in memory of Mary Shord.

Also two Chalices & a Paten in Britannia metal undated by Pratt & Sons London.

Two Ciboria, one pewter & one stainless steel.

The most important of these are the chalice and paten of 1846 and 1854. This chalice is illustrated here. It is a twelve sided cup with one apostle in a niche on each face. Around the stem and foot is an entwining serpent. This is to recall the legend of St John and the poisoned chalice, where the poison is represented by the serpent. The paten is similar in design with twelve apostles radiating from the centre and a serpent entwined stem. They are fine examples of the silversmiths craft and although given at different dates both were probably made at the same time by Angels of London.

The Lost Treasures

One of the important treasures of the church - the window on the south side of the chancel which was the work of Pugin from glass by Hardman. It was one of Pugin's best works. Its two panels depicted Christ and Martha -"Thy brother shall rise again" and Christ and the nobleman -"Thy son liveth" with a vivid palm tree over the top. It was in memory of Peter, only son of Peter and Annie Cox, who died at Bekfeya in the Lebanon on 11th Sep. 1850 aged 23 yrs and commemorated by a brass plaque on the sill of the window. This was easily the most valuable window in the church and was thrown out in the early 1970s. No faculty has been found for this act only a faculty to repair lead on the windows. There is no mention of it in P.C.C. minutes. To add insult to injury it was replaced with a plain window with square panes in contrast to the diamond panes of the rest of the church. About the same time the carved stone three-bay reredos of the altar, although less valuable, was also ripped out. The reason given was to let more light into the chancel but there was electric lighting and at one time there were roof windows which could have been reinstated.

The early church silver was "lost" during the Reformation when Beaminster was allowed to keep the worst of two chalices, which later disappeared. One chalice with a weight of 7oz and other ornaments to the value of 8s - 4d were seized from the St. Juthware chantry in 1547. Many of the seizures did not reached the crown coffers but graced the sideboards of state officials, just as looted vestments and altar frontals served them as bedspreads and table cloths. In 1652 two large silver tankards were purchased. Churchwardens accounts show that they paid 00 - 18s -8d for fourteen quarts of wine to fill them for two sacraments. These were, no doubt,

The Exeter Chandelier

used at Easter, which being a Day of Obligation, everyone was expected to attend the Eucharist. By the eighteenth century these tankards had disappeared.

Finally we consider the loss of the great chandelier and the corona. The writer is greatly indebted to Robert Sherlock a specialist in coronas for important information. A widow, Sarah Day of Beaminster, provided in her will for the gift of a chandelier to the church. Her will was proved on June 15th 1803 (Prerogative Court of Canterbury, 526 Marriott). It reads:

"I give and bequeath unto my Executor and Executrixes hereinafter named the Sum of Thirty Pounds upon this special Trust and confidence that they or the Survivors or Survivor of them do and shall as soon after my Decease as conveniently can be lay out the same or as much thereof as may necessary in the purchase of a neat brass Chandelier for the use of the Parish Church of Beaminster aforesaid with as many Branches thereto as they or the Survivors or Survivor of them shall think proper. And I do direct that my Name and the time of my Death and that it was my Gift may be engraved thereon and that my Executor and Executrixes or the Survivors or Survivor of them (with the consent of the Vicar or Minister of the said Parish Church of Beaminster and the Churclwardens thereof) do cause the same to be hung up in the said Church as nearly opposite the Ministers reading Desk as shall be thought proper there to remain for the use of the said Church for ever and it is my will and meaning that the said brass Chandelier and the Chain and furniture with which the same shall be hung up together with the Carriage thereof and all incidental Expenses shall bo borne and paid by and out of the said Sum of Thirty Pounds."

According to Hine (The History of Beaminster, 1914, pp 57-8) the chandelier was duly installed, suspended by a chain from the roof of the nave. It consisted of two brass globes with 24 branches. (Hine is certainly in error in stating 26). The lower globe carried a dove, (Hine calls it an eagle), with a scroll in its beak carrying the inscription, "The gift of Sarah Day of Beaminster, who died 27th March 1803". No photograph now exists but what is probably a very similar chandelier can be seen in Exeter Guildhall signed by Thomas Pryke of Bridgewater. However Samuel Flood became vicar in 1849 and in 1851 he had the chandelier taken down and cast as lumber into the Mort House. The townspeople were vexed and opposition grew. This was expressed in the following verses that were printed and circulated in the town:

Some years ago as I've heard say,
There lived a lady named Day

Her pious soul to God was bent
And to the church she always went
To prove her piety sincere
She gave to the church a chandelier
And there it hung - a pleasing sight
Untouched, except to keep it bright
Until of late there came a Flood
Who took it from the House of God,
And where it's gone I cannot say
That splendid gift of Lady Day.

At a vestry meeting on 13th August 1852 it was decided "That a communication to be made by the present Churchwardens to the Outgoing Churchwardens as to the removal of the chandelier from the church and to know where the same now is." On 17th September following the proposal was carried "that the Chandelier be properly cleaned and affixed in its old position." (Draft Vestry Minutes archived in Dorset County Record office). However in the 1862-3 restoration it was removed and recast into a corona lucis, A & E Toleman being the intermediaries. They gave £5 for the 200lb (approx) of brass. The corona made by Hart & Son was of three tiers and hung from chains in the chancel. It carried 36 gas jets and the dove and inscription from the chandelier. This was later also removed, reduced to a single tier with four gas lamps and hung in the Mort House. In 1959 Mr Sherlock wrote to Mr W.J. Bailey about the corona. The letter in reply shows that it was in the Mort House but enclosed a photograph showing the full corona in the chancel before the screen was erected. Mr Bailey states that the glass plates and prints made by Richard Hine were thrown out when his house was sold. Mr Bailey managed to save a few, of which this was one, and the remainder went to the refuse dump. In 1971 Mr Sherlock made inquiries of Canon Galloway about the corona, of which, according to the letters, Canon Galloway was trying to dispose He made a photograph of the corona in the Mort House. Further correspondence ensued and the matter was referred to the Diocesan Advisory Committee. A letter from Canon Galloway on 21st February 1973 shows that they were not adverse to the corona being placed in the County Museum. The museum did not have room at that time but was about to move into larger premises. However the corona did not get to the museum. A reminder was sent to Canon Galloway on March 2nd 1973. Nothing further was heard and the corona "disappeared", save for an entry at the end of P.C.C. minutes which reads, "sold scrap brass £5". When electricity replaced gas in the church in 1949 the nave lighting, amongst other gas lights, was swept away. The nave lights were carried on fluted brass standards which spread into a trifoliate design of wrought iron at the top. From the centre of each of these three scrolls hung a pendant gas light with bell shaped glass shade. There was one of these standards at the end of every third pew on both sides of the nave. No attempt, apparently, was made to keep these artistic standards and equip them with electric lights.

No faculty exists nor was application ever made for any of these actions. The history of these artefacts shows clearly that the faculty system offers little protection since it can be evaded. It raises the question whether the system of church government is capable of the proper care of our heritage despite the fact that PCCs usually include some alert and knowledgeable members. It may be that English Heritage will be the saviour.

Recent Changes

The later part of the twentieth century saw further changes in the ordering of the church. In 1951 it was decided that the choir stalls needed renewal, because of their age and also because the choir was now smaller. The work was carried out by W.J. Bailey & Sons at a cost of £252 16s 11d. In the 1960s the Church had decided that the priest should face the congregation during the Eucharist not having his back to them at the high altar, as had been the case. Further it was felt that the people should be able to witness the action of the Eucharist with the importance of its symbolism. To this end in Beaminster in 1964 a few pews were removed at the entrance to the chancel and a nave altar established there.

In 1964 the plinth, all that remained of the memorial gun in the Square was demolished, the plaques carrying the names of those who fought in World War I being removed. Following the granting of a faculty these were embedded in the churchyard wall at the 'church plane'.

1970 saw a further change. Some pews were removed from the east end of the north aisle and the north altar established. The pulpit was moved to the south aisle and the old lectern replaced. New altar rails, candlesticks and lectern were made at the Comprehensive School. At this time Beaminster became part of a Team Ministry. This consisted of fifteen churches in nine parishes with a Rector and two Vicars. All the glebe land and the vicarage was sold and a new rectory built.. However over the next few years three village churches, previously in other parishes, became parishes in their own right - Mosterton (1981), Drimpton (1982),and Salway Ash (1984). Further bench pews were removed to create a space by the War Memorial and to provide room for a bookcase.

In 1983 came the greatest change. The wooden floor, of the Canon Codd 'restoration', in the south aisle began to give way. Part of the aisle had to be closed to the public and it was found that the wood was infested with beetle as were some of the pews that had had to be removed. There was a danger that this infestation would get into the screen and the roof timbers. So the wooden floor was removed and all the pews. The floor was replaced with manufactured stone pavers similar to those originally in the church. One hundred and fifty upholstered chairs of beech were purchased to seat the congregation together with two hundred plastic stacking chairs for those occasions when more seating was required. This had several advantages. It provided flexibility so that the church could be used in various ways for concerts etc. Different configurations were also possible for particular forms of service. For example one ordination was held with the whole church131 in the round. It was also found that it was much cleaner; the old pews made thorough cleaning impossible and in addition the heat circulated better.

In 1993 a further improvement took place. The mort house and western arches had rather unsightly curtains. These were replaced with folding wooden screens designed by the architect Mr A.J. Harvey. English Heritage required that all this work should be of matching English oak. With some difficulty this requirement was met. This provided an opportunity to incorporate a concealed rolled steel girder in the upper part of the screen in the western arch for increased stability. At the same time matching wardrobes and cupboards were provided, which included housing for choir robes under the tower, and in the mort house. A donor provided a new oak screen to separate the mort house from the under tower space and the west door of the mort house which had been blocked up in 1887 by Hanns Builders was opened, restored, and a new oak door fitted in keeping with the rest of the church.

In these latter years there was another problem. There was no proper place to keep the sacrament when it was reserved for administration to the sick. Although lay people and readers could be licensed to administer the communion there was on occasion no priest to perform the consecration. In fact at one time there was, for some weeks, only one vicar for the whole team. An aumbry was, therefore, provided by a donor in February 2000 which could be an essential facility in years to come.

Appendix i
SOME SOURCES

Churchwardens Accounts.   )
Churchwardens Papers (Church Restorations)   ) Dorset
Canon Codd's collected letters.   ) County
Canon Codd's Diaries.   ) Record
Vestry Papers.   ) Office
Parochial Church Council Minutes.   )
The Register of St Osmund. Wiltshire Record Office.
Historia et Cartularium Monasterii Sancti Petri Gloucestriae.
    Gloucester Cathedral Register 'A'.
Proceedings Dorset Archaeological and Natural History   Society.
Barlow F. 'The English Church' 1000 - 1066.
Bond. F. 'Screens and Galleries in English Churches'. 1908.
Brocklehurst R.G. 'Some Dorset Church Towers'.
Clifton Taylor A. 'English Parish Churches as Works of Art'. 1974.
Darlington. R.R. 'The Vita Wulfstani of William of Malmesbury'.
Davis R.C. 'Mediaeval Cartularies of Gt Britain'. 1958.
Gallyon. M. 'The Early Church in Wessex & Mercia'. 1980.
Hart. W.H. 'Gloucester Cartularies' Rolls series (1863-67).
Hine. R. 'History of Beaminster'. 1914.
Jenkins S. 'England's Thousand Best Churches'. 1999.
Macray. Rev. D. 'Charters & Documents re History of cathedral city &
    diocese of Salisbury'.
Moorman. Rt. Rev. Bishop. J.R.H. 'The History of the Church in
    England'.
Rich-Jones W.H. ed. 'Register of St Osmund' (Rolls Series).
Sawyer P.H. 'Anglo-Saxon Charters'. 1968.
Sims-Williams. P. 'Religion & Literature in Western England'.
Talbot C.H. 'The Life of Saint Wulsin of Sherborne by Goscelin' in
    The Revue Benedictine.
Wakeman H.O. 'History of the Church of England'. 1896.

Appendix ii
A BRIEF GLOSSARY

aumbry	a secure cupboard for the storage of consecrated material
charnel house	place where bones removed from the churchyard are stored
corbel	block of stone which projects from a wall to support a roof beam or arch
cornice	a projecting horizontal moulding on a wall or column
corona	form of circular chandelier usually of several tiers carrying lights around each rim
crenellated	having a row of battlements
crocketed	bunched floral decoration on sides of pinnacles
cusps	small projecting point at the intersection of arcs in stone tracery
decalogue	wall fixture displaying the Ten Commandments, Lord's Prayer and/or the Creed
hagioscope	opening provided so that the main altar can be seen from outside the chancel sometimes called a squint
hatchment	diamond shaped painting, usually on board of the arms or family crest of a deceased person

hoi polloi	the many, the rabble, the vulgar
label stop	carved end to the ornamental stone hood of a doorway, window, etc.
ledger stone	large flat slab over a grave often let into the floor of a church
merlons	the raised sections of the battlements
modes	a charge on a parcel of land payable to a charity
monoxylon	chest made from hollowed out tree trunk
mortmain	Act of Parliament controlling property given to religious houses and institutions
ossuary	alternative name for charnel house
P.C.C.	the Parochial Church Council
paterae	band of square decorations e.g. around a tower
pilaster	narrow rectangular column built into but partly projecting from a wall
piscina	a niche containing a bowl or drain used in the washing of vessels from an altar
plinth	the stone base of a column, pinnacle, wall or pedestal
putti	young boys, often winged, depicted in sculptures
quatrefoil	tracery in the form of a four petalled flower

respond	half pillar that is built against the wall at the end of an arcade
rood	a crucifix, the cross of Christ
rood loft	gallery on top of chancel screen carrying the rood
sequester	to confiscate, but subject to future restoration
soffit	the underside of an arch
spall	a splinter of stone shed from the surface of a block usually due to weathering
springer stone	stone supporting a pinnacle
stoup	a basin used to hold holy water
tabula	a table like structure fixed to a wall or horizontal surface often the base of a monument
theophany	a manifestation of God to Man
tracery	perforated ornamental stonework in a window, screen, etc.

St. Osmund's Charter

Appendix iii
CARTA OSMUNDI

St Osmund's Charter dates from the early 11th century, but the present charter is not the original, but a copy made in the early 13th century. It is in contracted Latin on vellum. Contracted Latin is a form of shorthand Latin common at the time. However the vellum has deteriorated badly so that the charter is now only barely readable. The first portion, shown opposite, has been subjected to computer assisted restoration. Care has been taken not to alter diacritical marks or correct the several incorrect contractions or spelling mistakes. The occasional sputter of the scribe's quill has also been left intact. The text expanded into normal Latin reads:

IN NOMINE SANCTUS ET INDIVIDUAE TRINITATIS Ego Osmundus Sarum ecclesiae episcopus, omnibus Christi fidelibus tam posteris notifico quam presentibus ad honorem Domini Jhu. Christi, sanctissimsaeque Mariae Virginis, et pro salute animarum Willielmi regis et uxoris suae reginae Matildae atque filii sui Willielmi regis Anglorum regni successoris, pro salute etiam animae meae ecclesiam Sarum me construxisse, et in ea canonicos constituisse, atque illis viventibus canonice bona ecclesiae ita sicut ipse optinueram libere et ut exigit regularis censura canonice in perpetuum concessisse; has scilicet villas preter militum terras, Eteminster, Aulton, Cerminister, Begminister, Niderbiri, Writelinton; ecclesiam de Scireburne cum tota decima ejusdem villae, et cum ceteris appendiciis, excepta monachorum decima et sepultura;

A translation, somewhat free to preserve the original meaning in modern English, gives:

In the name of the holy and undivided Trinity I Osmond, Bishop of the church of Sarum, faithful to Christ in all things, and especially for the instruction of posterity, present this to the honour of Lord Jesus Christ, most holy Virgin Mary and subject to the will of King William,

King of England, and his wife Queen Matilda, also his son William and his ruling successors, subject also to my intention in building the Church of Sarum and established laws, also the present regulations for the good of the church, demand by the authority vested (in me) that the following be handed over in perpetuity, with, of course their manors and attached lands, Yetminster, Alton, Charminster, Beaminster, Netherbury, Writhlington, the Church of Sherborne with all its manorial tithes and the rest of its appurtenances. Except monastic tithes and burial fees . . .

ROYAL COMMISSION ON HISTORIC MONUMENTS RECORD
Also published by F.P. Pitfield in 'Dorset Parish Churches' (1981)

ST 4701/4801
11-11-66
7/32
GV
BEAMINSTER   CHURCH STREET
                                              (SOUTH SIDE)

St Mary's Church

Parish Church. C13, C15 and C16. Nave, north and south aisles, chancel, north east chapel, west tower, south west vestry, north porch. Rubble-stone and ashlar walls, ashlar dressings. Stone slate and lead roofs. C13: east end of north aisle wall, formerly end wall of C13 north transept. C15: north and south aisles, chancel rebuilt. Nave and aisles of 5 bays with 3-light stone mullions with panel tracery in pointed heads. Each bay with a short buttress. Window to organ-chamber, 4 lights with cusped trefoil ogees. Tracery with flattened quatrefoils under a 4-centred head. Plain parapets. Chancel: 2 bays east windows of 5 cinque-foiled lights with vertical tracery over. South wall with 2 C15 windows and a priest's doorway. North chapel, rebuilt 1505 by John Hillary of Meerhay. East window, of 4 cinquefoiled ogee lights, modern tracery in a 3-centred head. West tower, early C16. 3 stages, set-back buttresses pinnacled. Course of quatrefoils, above plinth, paterae above first string, coupled bell-openings in top stage and crenellated parapet. Sculpture in tiers: Virgin and Child, flanking niches. Crucifixion, Resurrection and Ascension with flanking figures, divided by crocketed pinnacles. All in second stage. Polygonal newel stair in north east corner fully pinnacled. North porch with diagonal buttresses, string and crenellated parapet, 1860's, Arch with moulded jambs and 4-centred head. South west vestry, mid C16, with reset windows.

Interior: Nave arcades, 2 west piers, C15, 2 east piers, C16. Conventional pier-design, 2-centred arches. Nave roof: arch-braced construction, renewed in C19. Crenellated wall-plate and one set of purlins. North and south aisles with pentice roof on carved head-stops, C.C17*

Chancel roof; also arch-braced C19. Chancel-arch, C15, 2-centred of one continuous moulded order. Soffit with double-panels, divided into tiers. Squint to south aisle. Fittings: font, late C12, Purbeck marble with square shallow bowl with round arcading on one side. Round stem with 4 colorettes. Piscinae: chancel, C14, north chapel with C20 cill, south aisle, C13 with trefoil ed head and gable. Pulpit: oak, octagonal with 2 tiers of arcaded panels, early C17. Brasses: 6 of C16, C17 and C18 date. Monuments: north aisle, to Danel Cox, 1778, John Cox 1783, Samuel Cox, 1801, brothers, white and grey marble wall monument put up in Samuel's lifetime, with shield-of-arms and standing female figure leaning on urn. 4 other marble wall monuments, including to Richard Symes, barrister, 1783 and family; oval medallion carved with female figure leaning on an urn. South aisle: •Strode monuments to Thomas Strode, Sergeant at Law 1698-9, marble with standing figure in wig, gown, side pilasters support cornice etc.

Appendix v

R.C.H.Ii. Dorset I, p 17(l)ff. P.P. Pitfield, Dorset Parish Churches (1981) pp 48-52.

ROYAL COMMISSION ON HISTORIC MONUMENTS

ST 4701/4801   BEAMINSTER   CHURCH STREET
                             (SOUTH SIDE)

7/33

7 Table Tombs in St Mary's Churchyard

GV

7 Table Tombs. (1) In angle of north porch and aisle wall. Stone with 2 panelled sides on each face. Dated 1707 on rear face. Very flattened ovolo-moulds. Heavy moulded cornice. (2) 8 yards north of porch, stone. that of Samuel Gox, died 1741. Panelled sides with modillions and heavy moulded cornice. (3) North east of porch by 6 yards, inscription illegible, fielded-panel. corners. (4) 7 yards west of tower, stone to Edward (?) Lockner, died 178-. Corners with 3 tiers of fielded panels (5) 10 yards north west of Tower, stone with flat ovolo panels, dated 1719. (6) 17 yards west of tower, with 3 tiers of fielded panels at corners, inscription illegible. Heavy cornice with low hipped top. Mid CI8. (7) In mid C18 style but to Thomas. Fox, Gentleman, died. 1859. Panels have (incorrect) straight-chamfered framing,
ST 4701/4801 ' BEAMINSTER

7/35
CHURCH STREET
(SOUTH STDE)

Churchyard Wall with attached gate-piers and ramp, 10 metres north east of Church

Churchyard Wall. C19 or earlier, c. 10 foot high and 40 yards long
Stone rubble wall, with stone-coping bounding churchyard on north side
Stone quatrefoil bands in between. Iron gates in style of piers
Attached stone ramp, c. C19 with stone cobble surface and stone sides
10 yards long leading up to the gates.
NOTE. Error - there are eight table tombs in St Mary's Churchyard.

Appendix vi
Survival of the Images

The survival of the images on the tower of St Mary's church presents a problem for historical research. The Cromwellian period began in 1649 and in 1653 the Images Act was passed requiring the destruction of images but the images in Beaminster were not destroyed. There are no empty niches on the tower and only two images have been replaced since the tower was built despite the fact that Beaminster had a small but militant group of dissenters. The reason sometimes given is that the images could not be reached. This cannot be true since there are several images at ground level and others could be reached using the postern door of the tower which leads on to the roof. Perhaps an answer can be found in considering the situation at the time. The town had been burnt down in 1644. Before that time images were sometimes removed from inside churches but not from outside. In fact anyone doing so would have received short shrift. Sprigge writing in 1645 describes the town as a mass of ivy covered ruins but makes no mention of any shanty town providing shelter for the refugees. We can only assume that the inhabitants had fled to surrounding villages, hamlets and farms. Rebuilding was still going on in 1660. So it may be that the dispersal of would be iconoclasts prevented damage being done to the images. It has been said that some puritans got to the top of the tower and damaged the pinnacles. Why then did they stop at that when there were easier targets available? Then again the two figures replaced in 1878 were up on the north-west buttress and it was thought that these niches were empty because of Cromwellian depredations. In view of the foregoing is this likely? We do not know and only the discovery of some so far uncatalogued document could provide an answer.

We shall not cease from exploration

And the end of all our exploring

Will be to arrive where we started

And to know the place for the first time.

George Elliot "Little Gidding"